ART IS A LIE
THAT MAKES US REALIZE TRUTH. —PABLO PICASSO

BLUE
MAN
WORLD

BLACK DOG
& LEVENTHAL
PUBLISHERS
NEW YORK

DESIGN BY EIGHT AND A HALF

BLACK DOG & LEVENTHAL PUBLISHERS
HACHETTE BOOK GROUP
1290 AVENUE OF THE AMERICAS
NEW YORK, NY 10104
WWW.HACHETTEBOOKGROUP.COM
WWW.BLACKDOGANDLEVENTHAL.COM

FIRST EDITION: OCTOBER 2016
BLACK DOG & LEVENTHAL PUBLISHERS IS AN IMPRINT OF
HACHETTE BOOKS, A DIVISION OF HACHETTE BOOK GROUP.
THE BLACK DOG & LEVENTHAL PUBLISHERS NAME AND
LOGO ARE TRADEMARKS OF HACHETTE BOOK GROUP, INC.

THE PUBLISHER IS NOT RESPONSIBLE FOR WEBSITES
(OR THEIR CONTENT) THAT ARE NOT OWNED BY THE PUBLISHER.
THE HACHETTE SPEAKERS BUREAU PROVIDES A WIDE RANGE
OF AUTHORS FOR SPEAKING EVENTS. TO FIND OUT MORE, GO TO
WWW.HACHETTESPEAKERSBUREAU.COM OR CALL (866) 376-6591.
ADDITIONAL CREDITS INFORMATION IS ON PAGE 206.

LIBRARY OF CONGRESS CATALOGING-IN-PUBLICATION DATA
HAS BEEN APPLIED FOR.

ISBN: 978-0-316-39518-2 (HARDCOVER),
978-0-316-39519-9 (EBOOK)
PRINTED IN THE UNITED STATES OF AMERICA
RRD-W

10 9 8 7 6 5 4 3 2 1

TABLE OF CONTENTS

(8) **INTRODUCTION**

SECTION 1
(10) **WHO ARE THE BLUE MEN?**

(10) **SIGHTINGS IN THE MODERN ERA**

(20) Blue Man Worldwide

(12) Blue Man Sightings in History: Unsubstantiated

(14) Funeral for the Eighties
(16) Manhattan

(22) **BLUE MAN ANATOMY**

(18) Growing Influence

(36) **BLUE MAN SENSES**

(22) Blue Genome Project

(26) Under the Skin

(30) Plumbing

(34) Blue Brain

(38) Sight

(24) The Body

(32) A Strange Beast

(40) Hearing and Receiving

(42) Touch

(28) Bald & Blue

(44) Taste/Smell

(46) Synesthesia

(48) **BLUE MAN BEHAVIOR**

(48) Modality Theory

(56) Tripartite Siphonophoric Theory

(58) Id/Superego Theory, AKA Freudian Theory

(60) Connectedness

(50) Scientist/Shaman

(52) Hero/Innocent

(54) Group Member/Trickster

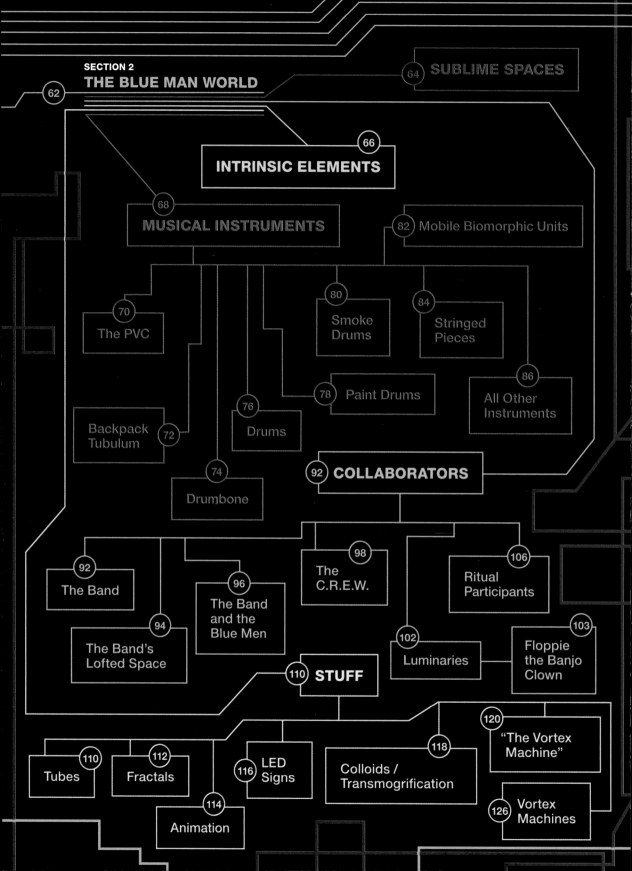

SECTION 2
THE BLUE MAN WORLD — 62

64 — SUBLIME SPACES

66 — **INTRINSIC ELEMENTS**

68 — **MUSICAL INSTRUMENTS**

82 — Mobile Biomorphic Units

70 — The PVC

80 — Smoke Drums

84 — Stringed Pieces

78 — Paint Drums

86 — All Other Instruments

72 — Backpack Tubulum

76 — Drums

74 — Drumbone

92 — **COLLABORATORS**

92 — The Band

96 — The Band and the Blue Men

98 — The C.R.E.W.

106 — Ritual Participants

94 — The Band's Lofted Space

102 — Luminaries

103 — Floppie the Banjo Clown

110 — **STUFF**

110 — Tubes

112 — Fractals

116 — LED Signs

118 — Colloids / Transmogrification

120 — "The Vortex Machine"

114 — Animation

126 — Vortex Machines

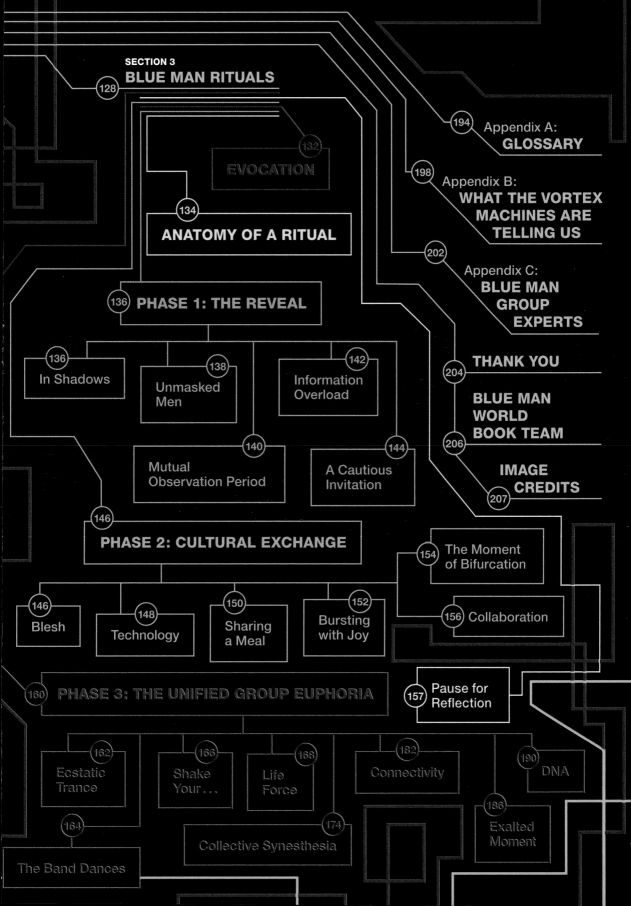

SECTION 3
BLUE MAN RITUALS — 128

EVOCATION — 132

ANATOMY OF A RITUAL — 134

PHASE 1: THE REVEAL — 136

In Shadows — 136

Unmasked Men — 138

Information Overload — 142

Mutual Observation Period — 140

A Cautious Invitation — 144

PHASE 2: CULTURAL EXCHANGE — 146

The Moment of Bifurcation — 154

Blesh — 146

Technology — 148

Sharing a Meal — 150

Bursting with Joy — 152

Collaboration — 156

Pause for Reflection — 157

PHASE 3: THE UNIFIED GROUP EUPHORIA — 160

Ecstatic Trance — 162

Shake Your... — 166

Life Force — 168

Connectivity — 182

DNA — 190

Collective Synesthesia — 174

Exalted Moment — 186

The Band Dances — 164

Appendix A: GLOSSARY — 194

Appendix B: WHAT THE VORTEX MACHINES ARE TELLING US — 198

Appendix C: BLUE MAN GROUP EXPERTS — 202

THANK YOU — 204

BLUE MAN WORLD BOOK TEAM — 206

IMAGE CREDITS — 207

A TRIO OF BALD AND BLUE MEN FIRST APPEARED
A QUARTER OF A CENTURY AGO WANDERING
THE STREETS OF NEW YORK CITY. SINCE THAT TIME,
THESE BLUE MEN HAVE BECOME A CULTURAL
PHENOMENON. THEIR RITUALISTIC HAPPENINGS HAVE
BEEN EXPERIENCED BY OVER 35 MILLION PEOPLE
IN MORE THAN FIFTEEN DIFFERENT COUNTRIES.

BUT WHO ARE THESE BLUE MEN? WHERE DO THEY
COME FROM? WHY HAVE THEY COME HERE?
WHY ARE THERE ONLY THREE OF THEM? WHY ARE
THEY ALWAYS TOGETHER? WHAT DRIVES THEIR
CURIOSITY? WHAT DO THEY HOPE TO ACCOMPLISH?

SINCE THE BLUE MEN CAN'T (OR WON'T) SPEAK,
THESE QUESTIONS REMAIN UNANSWERED.
EVIDENCE AND CONJECTURE HAS BEEN GATHERED
FROM HUNDREDS OF EXPERTS IN THE FIELDS OF
SCIENCE, ART, ANTHROPOLOGY, ETHNOMUSICOLOGY,
BIOLUMINESCENCE, PSYCHOLOGY, CIVIL
ENGINEERING, NEUROSCIENCE, PARTICLE PHYSICS,
RHEOLOGY, AND MOLECULAR GASTRONOMY.[1]

THE FOLLOWING OBSERVATIONS ARE AN ATTEMPT
TO EXCAVATE BLUE MAN GROUP'S WORLD IN
SEARCH OF THE TRUTH.

① Also consulted were experts in chaos theory, comic book theory, conspiracy theory, and theory theory.

SECTION 1
WHO ARE THE BLUE MEN?

THE EXACT ORIGINS OF BLUE MAN GROUP ARE A MYSTERY,[1] THEREFORE GENERATING AN ETHNOHISTORY[2] IS A CHALLENGE. HOWEVER, SCIENTIFIC OBSERVATION AND ANECDOTAL EVIDENCE CAN GIVE US IMPORTANT INSIGHT INTO WHO THE BLUE MEN ARE AND HOW THEY TOOK ON A MYSTERIOUS ROLE IN OUR OWN CULTURE.

①Much like Area 51, the Bermuda Triangle, the assassination of JFK, Stonehenge, the glyphs of Rongorongo, and the mystery of consciousness.ˮ ②Anthropologists develop an ethnohistory to explore how the historical record can inform the study of a subject. From the Greek *ethnos*, meaning "nation" and *historia*, "finding out, narrative." ³According to Neuroscientist V. S. Ramachandran, "Any single brain, including yours, is made up of atoms that were forged in the hearts of countless, far-flung stars billions of years ago. These particles drifted for eons and light-years until gravity and chance brought them together here, now. These atoms now form a conglomerate— your brain—that can not only ponder the very stars that gave it birth but can also think about its own ability to think and wonder about its own ability to wonder. With the arrival of humans, it has been said, the universe has suddenly become conscious of itself. This, truly, is the greatest mystery of all."

BLUE MAN SIGHTINGS IN HISTORY:
UNSUBSTANTIATED

1735
waterskiing in Venice with Canaletto

15,000 BC
in Lascaux Cave Paintings

1664 New Amersterdam
is renamed New York.

1793
in northern North America
with Big Foot

3000 BC building
of the Great Pyramid.

NUMEROUS WITNESSES CLAIM to have seen a trio
of Blue Men prior to 1988, but due to lack of
evidence, such claims cannot be corroborated.

1509-1511
hanging out in The School of Athens
as recorded by Raphael.

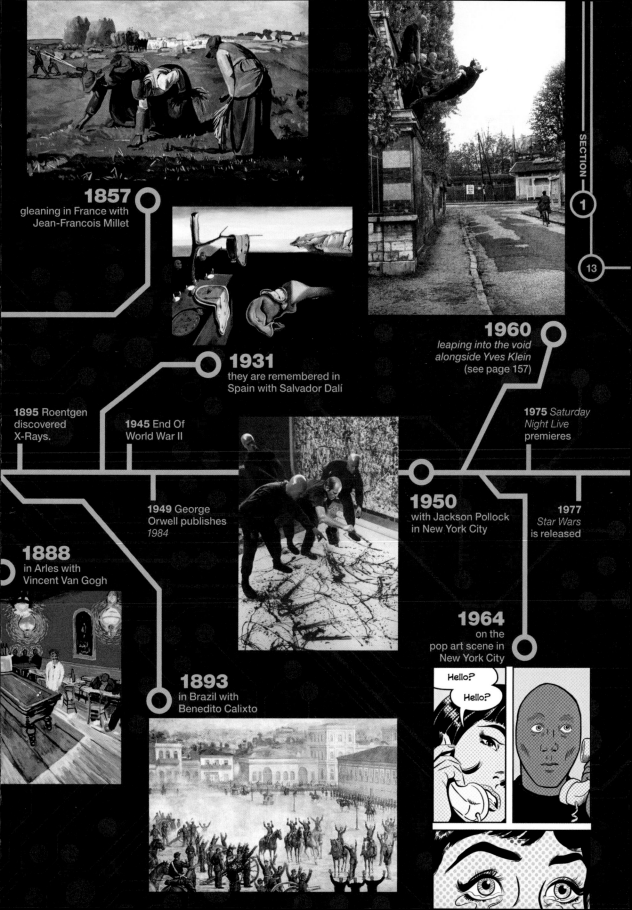

1857
gleaning in France with
Jean-Francois Millet

1931
they are remembered in
Spain with Salvador Dalí

1960
*leaping into the void
alongside Yves Klein
(see page 157)*

1895 Roentgen
discovered
X-Rays.

1945 End Of
World War II

1975 *Saturday
Night Live*
premieres

1949 George
Orwell publishes
1984

1950
with Jackson Pollock
in New York City

1977
Star Wars
is released

1888
in Arles with
Vincent Van Gogh

1964
on the
pop art scene in
New York City

1893
in Brazil with
Benedito Calixto

Hello?

Hello?

SIGHTINGS IN THE MODERN ERA: FUNERAL FOR THE EIGHTIES

THE FIRST SUBSTANTIATED SIGHTING of the Blue Men dates back to 1988 in New York City's Central Park. Witnesses claim to have seen a number of bald, blue men participating[1] in a "Funeral for the Eighties."[2] A number of items representing iconic eighties totems, including the yuppie, *Rambo*-ism, postmodern architecture,[3] and "cheesy" eighties music videos were placed in a coffin and buried. Some observers believe this funeral illustrated a collective desire to move beyond a decade of self-indulgent excess and very bad hair.[4] Still, other witnesses contend the people in these photographs are not Blue Men at all, but rather a group of superfans attempting to create their own Blue Man Group. *(see The Blue Man Insiders Movement)*

NEW WAVE IS OLD.

PUNK IS A PATENTED FASHION OPTION.

'Postmodernism' is a ~~TYPE~~ term used in Elle magazine to describe parkas.

The club scene is dead.
Audiences sit and watch bands strike the same "new" poses.

The Reagan Era

is over.

The ~~FIX~~ yuppies have crashed.
It's time, past time, to renew.
TIME TO REINVENT OURSELVES.

Time to get a running start into the

'90s & LEAVE THIS DECADE BEHIND.

ITEM FOUND AT THE SCENE

14

THE BLUE MAN INSIDERS MOVEMENT

Since the earliest sightings of the trio, people have experimented with dressing up as Blue Men. Today, these people are recognized as members of a movement called Blue Man Insiders.[5]

Anthropologist and Blue Man expert Erdal Atintop says, "The Blue Man Insiders are a fascinating subculture. Some of the Insiders study the Blue Men seriously, in order to see the world as they do." Early Insider Manny Harris explains, "We aim to learn all we can about the universe by imitating the Blue Man in body, mind, and spirit."[6] Other more casual believers occasionally dress up as Blue Men for fun, as a type of cosplay.[7]

While not an academic document, the Blue Man Insiders handbook *The Conduit: Becoming Blue* has become a source of constant fascination for scholars in the field of Blue Man studies.

SECTION 1

15

[1]It has been speculated that the Blue Men did not arrange this happening, but simply joined an event already in progress. Experts disagree as to whether the Blue Men genuinely hate the 1980s or simply enjoy symbolic pop culture funerals. [2]If only they had thought to hold this event ten years earlier, the world might have been spared that horrific decade. [3]Specifically, the AT&T Building (now the Sony Building). [4]

[5]Particularly active Blue Man Insider* circles are thought to exist in Boston, Chicago, Las Vegas, New York, Orlando, Berlin, and on Blue Man Insider tours that reach across the globe. [6]Harris's statement was issued via a self-programmed scrolling LED sign. Like many die-hard[†] Blue Man Insiders, Harris does not often speak out loud. [7]Cosplay: from "costume" and "play." Starting in the 1990s, fans of anime and comic book culture began costuming themselves as their favorite characters. Today cosplay is an integral part of comic book conventions. Though a Blue Man ritual differs significantly from Comic-Con,[‡] both address the need for shared experience that allows people to overcome the urban isolation that is slowly but steadily sapping the world of all meaningful human interaction. *Nicknames include "Blue Believers," "Blue Man Groupies," or simply, "Bloupies." [†]Perhaps the most die-hard Blue Man Insiders are the trio known as Chris, Matt, and Phil, or "CMP" for short. Collectively, they represent over seventy-five years worth of intense study of the Blue Man character. For more information, see page 202. [‡]Comic-Con: a series of rituals particular to the comic book subculture that has taken on an outsize importance to the culture at large. (Due to large numbers of cosplayers, some consider Comic-Con part book fair, part convention, half Nerdy Gras.)

SIGHTINGS
IN THE
MODERN ERA:
MANHATTAN

FOLLOWING THE CENTRAL PARK APPEARANCE, there were regular reports of three Blue Men roaming the streets of New York City. Witnesses claim the Blue Men expressed particular interest in flow distribution systems, both liquid and informational. Hydrologist Bertrand Johanson[1] has stated publicly that "the Blue Men were particularly fascinated by the modern plumbing system, in which water flows from a reservoir to aqueducts and viaducts, to pipes, and finally to faucets before falling into glass drinking vessels. They would observe with fascination as said vessels transported water into the human mouth and then was shuttled through an internal decomposition system before releasing it through one of two outlet ports into porcelain retrieval vessels, which then drained into the plumbing system before being released into large bodies of water that finally resupply the reservoir system in a mind bogglingly elegant, never-ending, Möbius strip-like system of regeneration."

The Blue Men's fascination with this complex system may help explain why the largest cluster of sightings took place at industrial plumbing supply stores on Canal Street.

MÖBIUS STRIP OR BAND (/ˈmɜːrbiəs/ (non-rhotic) or US/moʊbiəs/; German:[ˈmøːbjʊs]), The Möbius strip or band is a surface with only one side and only one boundary, with the mathematical property of being non-orientable. It was discovered independently by the German mathematicians August Ferdinand Möbius and Johann Benedict Listing in 1858.

While most Blue Man sightings occurred in Manhattan, less-frequently acknowledged locations including Houston, New Orleans, Milwaukee, Minneapolis, Manchester[2] and, ~~inexplicably~~ interestingly, Cleveland.[3]

[1]From the world-renowned think tank Kazakhstan Institute for Strategic Studies (KISS). [2]A Manchester street vendor recalls selling a mix tape,* including The KLF's "Last Train to Trancentral,"[†] to three Blue Men. This song could later be heard during the climax of certain Blue Man rituals. [3]Everyone's always dumping on Cleveland.[‡] *Mix tapes were cassette tapes[§] that had songs from several different albums on them, "mixed" together. [†] The KLF is a British acid house punk band of the late 1980s and early 1990s. [‡]But then again, it is Cleveland…[§]Cassette tapes were a music delivery system created by the music industry** to replace LPs[††]. **The music industry used to exist. [††]Anyone unaware of what an "LP" is should ask their parents or a millennial.

At this time, the Blue Men were also observed in television sets around the world. Descriptions of these occurrences vary so greatly it is difficult to pinpoint exactly what they were doing and why.

SIGHTINGS IN THE MODERN ERA: GROWING INFLUENCE

WHILE THE EARLIEST modern-era Blue Man sightings usually occurred in intimate spaces with few witnesses, by 2006, as word of their existence spread, progressively larger crowds flocked to experience the Blue Man scene. As small gatherings of devotees ballooned to stadium-filling throngs of fans, the Blue Men sought guidance from a step-by-step manual that allowed them to enact the particular western ritual known as the "rock concert."①

ORDER NOW!   Only ①

① This rock concert manual* was made available to the general public for a limited time only. *For visual examples of rock concert movements, see page 105.

SIGHTINGS IN THE MODERN ERA: BLUE MAN WORLDWIDE

AS OF THIS WRITING, Blue Man Group has been known to host ritualistic happenings for everyone from the Queen of England to Tobias Fünke[1] and from Penn all the way to Teller.

Blue Man enthusiast Hazel DeWitt,[2] recently waxed poetic as she speculated on their appeal saying, "As the world becomes smaller and flatter, as traditional societies disintegrate and new technologies hijack our waking thoughts and fracture our attention spans, the isolation and loneliness of modern urban life become increasingly all-pervasive. In their ritualistic happenings, the Blue Men call forth an euphoric collective gestalt. We seek this out. We yearn for it. These ritualistic happenings are nothing less than the shattered pieces of the world attempting to glue themselves back together."

Others disagree.[3]

IF YOU BELIEVE YOU HAVE SEEN BLUE MAN GROUP ANYWHERE ELS

① Tobias Fünke became a cultural figure in 2003 when his wife's family, the Bluths, was profiled by reality television series *Arrested Development*. Due to its fast pace and amusing narration, *Arrested Development* is frequently mistaken for a scripted comedy series. Tobias's obsession with becoming a member of Blue Man Group is often cited as proof that the series is a documentary and not a comedy, as it is exceedingly believable and clearly not at all funny.
② Director of Performance Studies at Tennessee University at Disco.*
③ Yumi Igarishi, student of performance studies at Tennessee University at Disco, currently under the tutelage of Hazel DeWitt, disagrees and plans to write her dissertation about it but she hasn't gotten around to it yet. *NB: "Disco" refers to an unincorporated community in Blount County, Tennessee, rather than a club with pulsating lights and a dance floor.

BLUE MAN ANATOMY: BLUE GENOME PROJECT

AN INITIAL COMPARISON between Blue Man
and human genetic code reveals an extraordinary likeness.
Of the many commonalities, the most profound similarity
lies deep within the strands of a shared DNA:
the primal need for connection with others.

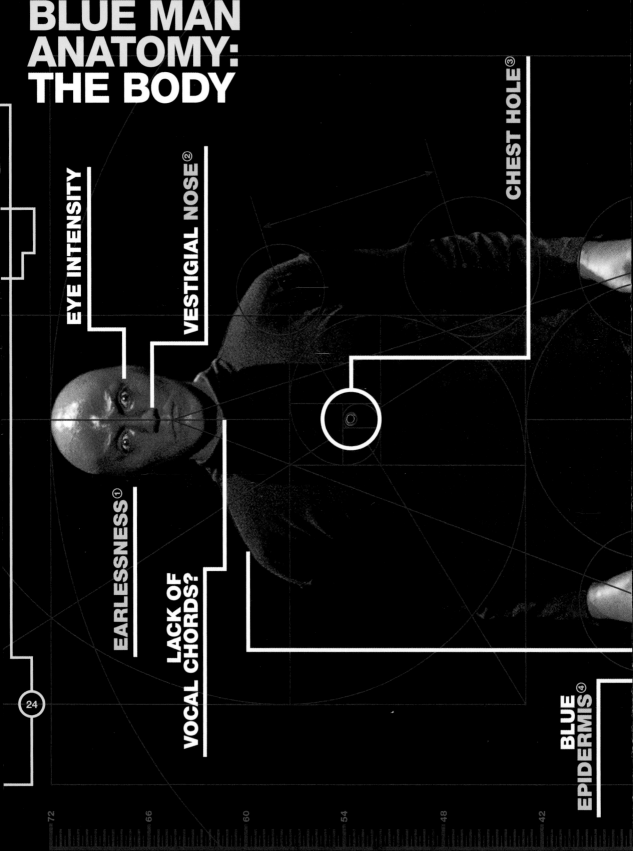

BLUE MAN ANATOMY: THE BODY

EYE INTENSITY

VESTIGIAL NOSE[2]

CHEST HOLE[3]

EARLESSNESS[1]

LACK OF VOCAL CHORDS?

BLUE EPIDERMIS[4]

72

66

60

54

48

42

CALLYPIGIAN BUTTOCKS⑤

①For more information on Blue Man Group's hearing ability, see page 40. ②It is believed the nose may have become functionless over the course of evolution. ③For more information on the chest hole (also known as the "Chanus"), see page 30. ④The complexion is a shade of Blue that is 100% saturated and 65% bright. Color theorists believe the hue to be a close match to either Pantone 2728C, or the Blue with hex value #002FA7, commonly known as "International Klein Blue." The epidermis ranges in texture from mirror-finish smooth to an irregular surface best described like an artist's oil paint brushstroke. ⑤Callipygian: shapely.

FOOT SIZE:
US 9,10
EU 43,44
UK 8,9

UNIFORMITY

BLUE MAN ANATOMY: UNDER THE SKIN

BLUE MAN ANATOMY: BALD & BLUE

ANY COMPARISON BETWEEN the Blue Men and humans would be incomplete without acknowledging the most conspicuous difference, their smooth blueness. The combination of glistening cobalt hue with smooth, hairless pate is not only considered sleek and sexy but also quite utilitarian, giving the Blue Men the same aerodynamic properties as racecars, rockets, or other streamlined objects.

The Blue Man Insiders' handbook *The Conduit: Becoming Blue* calls out this similarity between the Blue Men and the Silver Surfer. Blue Man expert Hans Swaerdens explains "for Silver Surfer, baldness does not equate with nakedness and vulnerability—quite the opposite. In his case, baldness is part of his persona as a 'superhero.' We think of the Blue Men as having both the commitment of a hero and the emotional nakedness of an innocent and we like to think that Blue Man Group's baldness helps to evoke both of these things simultaneously."

This archival photograph suggests that the Blue Men may in fact exhibit smooth blueness all over, however, the validity of this suggestion can not be substantiated.

BUTOH DANCERS

Like the Blue Men, the Butoh dancers move with singular purpose and don't speak.
Unlike the Blue Men, they are often seen almost totally nude whereas Blue Men dress entirely in black regardless of the formality of the event.

PORTUGUESE MAN-OF-WAR

(AKA THE BLUEBOTTLE, THE FLOATING TERROR)
The man-of-war's ability to "breathe" under water is the only differentiation of note.

LITTLE RED CORVETTE

Like the Blue Men, it is sleek, fast, and aerodynamic.
Unlike the Blue Men, it's red.

CHICAGO BEAN

Like the Blue Men, it reflects the world around it, attracts crowds, and has the appearance of liquid mercury.
Unlike the Blue Men, it is a piece of public art by Anish Kapoor located in the heart of Chicago's Millennium Park.

SILVER SURFER

Like the Blue Men, he is a smooth, hairless, simply dressed man who often operates in the mode of the hero. Unlike the Blue Men, he's a metallic-skinned humanoid comic superhero who soars through space on a surfboard that can travel faster than light and who started out as a herald serving an evil devourer of planets named Galactacus, but was converted to the side of goodness by the Fantastic Four.

BLUE M&M'S

Like the Blue Men, they have a smooth blue shell.
Unlike the Blue Men, blue M&M's usually appear in groups larger than three.

DWAYNE "THE ROCK" JOHNSON

Like the Blue Men, he is powerful and charismatic.
Unlike the Blue Men, he is powerful and charismatic.

BLUE MAN ANATOMY: PLUMBING

THE EXISTENCE OF A "CHEST HOLE" in Blue Man anatomy is one of the most curious yet rarely studied anatomical characteristics.

Dr. Leonard Chanus (chā-nəs), the scientist most often credited for the discovery of this supplemental digestive tract (and for whom it is named), believes the Chanus serves a dual function—one digestive, the other expressive. "Compared to humans, the Blue Men possess an auxiliary digestive system, which is elevated and accelerated. Matter enters through the mouth and may rapidly exit through the Chanus. While the human intestines are roughly twenty-five feet long, the Blue Men appear to have a digestive tract the length of an average piccolo."

He continues, "The most astonishing function of the Chanus is its ability to explode with emotion. The Blue Man anatomy illustrates the beauty of an open system.[1] The Blue Men are inexplicably able to take in multi-sensory information—life force[2], energy, vibes, whatever you want to call it—and as the input grows and expands, the Blue Men literally burst with joy."

Dr. Chanus's colleagues have periodically proposed alternative names for the Chanus. Some of the less universally accepted names are: the nozzle (or "the noz," for short), spew spot, the winner's circle, mystery spot, flugelhorn, the Leonard.

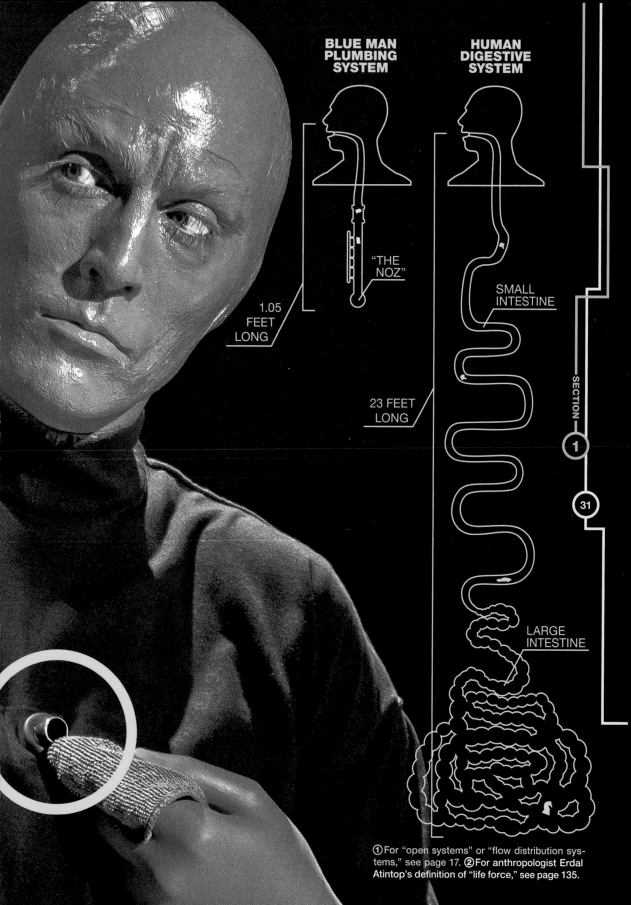

BLUE MAN
PLUMBING
SYSTEM

HUMAN
DIGESTIVE
SYSTEM

"THE NOZ"

1.05 FEET LONG

23 FEET LONG

SMALL INTESTINE

LARGE INTESTINE

SECTION

1

31

① For "open systems" or "flow distribution systems," see page 17. ② For anthropologist Erdal
Atintop's definition of "life force," see page 135.

BLUE MAN ANATOMY: A STRANGE BEAST

FOXES
Tricksy, adorable, nobody knows what they say

WOODPECKERS
Percussive, headbangers

NARWHALS
Hard to believe they really exist

SHEEP
Will follow anyone playing music

BASED ON THE aforementioned studies, most experts agree that of all the creatures in the animal kingdom, Blue Men are *most* similar to humans. However, experts are split as to how exactly to define the differences between Blue Man and human.

Professor of comparative anatomy Dr. Maria Shelley has joined forces with Director of the Center for Primate Behavior Dr. Lucy S. Diamond to compare Blue Men to other animals. What can viewing the Blue Men through the lens of other species teach us about them?

BEAVERS
Social, busy, interested in construction, especially as it relates to influencing the flow of liquid

DOLPHINS
Smooth skin, good at flips, the camera loves them

Blue Men also share several traits in common with newborn human babies—they are innocent, nonjudgmental, strangely compelling, induce huge surges of oxytocin, and excrete explosively.

DOGS
Good at catching things in their mouths; understand more than you think

SIPHONOPHORES
Single animals made of
separate organisms

CHIMPANZEES
Groom each other
with heightened
efficacy and care

BIRDS
Of a feather
flock together

PANDAS
You want to hug
them but you don't
know why

WHALES
Musical, hear with their
whole bodies

TAPIRS
You know why

HIPPOS
Excrete an oily
substance that covers
their skin

SYNCHRONOUS
FIREFLIES
Express themselves through
luminescence, build simultaneous
actions from just a few fireflies to
millions of fireflies flashing together
in a massive gestalt

BLIND MICE
Travel in groups of three;
have no tails

MANTIS SHRIMP
See colors humans will never perceive

BLUE MAN ANATOMY: BLUE BRAIN

PARIETAL LOBE

MOTOR CORTEX

BASAL GANGLIA

CORPUS CALLOSUM

AMYGDALA

THALAMUS

FRONTAL CORTEX

HIPPOCAMPUS

FRONTAL LOBE

PRIMARY VISUAL CORTEX

OCCIPITAL LOBE

OPTIC TRACT

HYPOTHALAMUS

INSULA

SUBSTANTIA NIGRA

PITUITARY GLAND

OLFACTORY BULB

CEREBELLUM

TEMPORAL LOBE

PONS

AQUEDUCT OF SYLVIUS

MEDULLA OBLONGATA

SPINAL CORD

Although increasingly rare in the scientific community, there are a few remaining hold-outs who cling to the homunculus theory as it applies to the Blue Men, believing the brain is "operated" by a puppet master in the form of a little man, or in this case, three little men.

HUMAN BRAIN

Evidence suggests that personal encounters with the Blue Men result in increased secretions of oxytocin in the observer, causing some to speculate that Blue Men are oxytocin rich themselves. Oxytocin, known anecdotally as the "happiness hormone," is a hormone which facilitates intimacy, bonding, and connection with other beings. It encourages a sense of well-being and the desire to spoon. It also aids in the labor and birthing process and lactation. It is unknown whether the Blue Men enjoy these benefits.

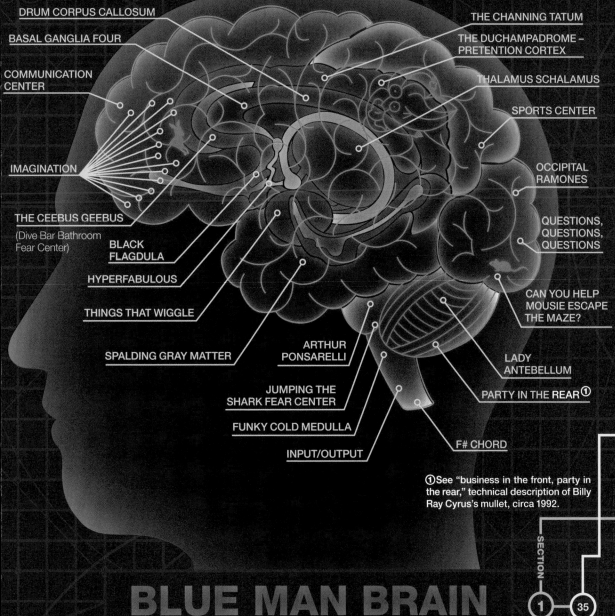

DRUM CORPUS CALLOSUM

BASAL GANGLIA FOUR

COMMUNICATION CENTER

IMAGINATION

THE CEEBUS GEEBUS
(Dive Bar Bathroom Fear Center)

BLACK FLAGDULA

HYPERFABULOUS

THINGS THAT WIGGLE

SPALDING GRAY MATTER

ARTHUR PONSARELLI

JUMPING THE SHARK FEAR CENTER

FUNKY COLD MEDULLA

INPUT/OUTPUT

THE CHANNING TATUM

THE DUCHAMPADROME – PRETENTION CORTEX

THALAMUS SCHALAMUS

SPORTS CENTER

OCCIPITAL RAMONES

QUESTIONS, QUESTIONS, QUESTIONS

CAN YOU HELP MOUSIE ESCAPE THE MAZE?

LADY ANTEBELLUM

PARTY IN THE REAR①

F# CHORD

①See "business in the front, party in the rear," technical description of Billy Ray Cyrus's mullet, circa 1992.

BLUE MAN BRAIN

BLUE MAN
SENSES

BLUE MAN SENSES: SIGHT

TO AN OUTSIDE OBSERVER, Blue Man's eyes appear anatomically indistinguishable from those of human beings. However, the intensity of their gaze has led a number of experts to speculate that the Blue Men might possess the ability to see the world differently.

What does the world look like through Blue Man Group's eyes? A number of hypotheses have been proposed:

Dr. Ludwig von Laibach believes that "the Blue Men see first and foremost the 'essence' of things. They do not necessarily see you, they see the energy you put out, they see your 'life force,' they see how you are connected to—or disconnected from—all living things."

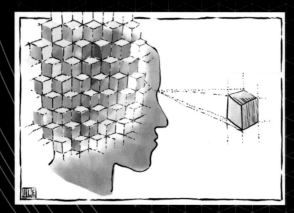

A more contested theory involves a rumor that Hugo Gernsback was on the brink of discovering the "Blue Man way of seeing" when he accidentally created the predecessor to Google Glass instead.[2]

Similarly, international art expert Joann Eckstut has theorized that "Blue Man Group's interest in art must stem from a heightened sensitivity to color and emotion. After all, who better understands the human spirit than the masters? My belief is that the Blue Men possess an ultra perceptive ability to see and appreciate not only the artwork itself, but the true feeling that stirred the impulse to create it."

Angelique Hildebrant is of the opinion that they "can see elements such as air, heat, and even sound waves. They likely take in music with their whole bodies including through their eyes and their taste buds. Can you imagine being able to taste Beethoven?"

Herpetologist Dr. Dylan Alter theorizes that Blue Man Group sight is more amphibious than human. "Take the frog, whose sight is connected to movement. When he is in motion, he sees everything. But when he is still, he can only see what is moving, what looks like dinner, which for him is an insect. He sees what he *needs* to see. The Blue Men are no different. Question is, what is it they *need* to see?"[1]

[1] Dr. Alter also posits that, like frogs, Blue Men possess a mirrored tissue layer in the eyes, called the tapetum lucidum or "eye shine," which allows them to reflect light in the dark.* [2] No evidence of this theory can be found.
*This theory was further explored in Alter's barely selling book, *Get Your Shine On: Finding Your Inner Frog on Your Path to True Happiness.*

SOUNDS LIKE
THE OCEAN

ACTUAL OCEAN

BLUE MAN SENSES:
HEARING AND
RECEIVING

THE BLUE MEN HAVE NO EARS. But this does not mean they cannot hear. In fact, some speculate that they can hear far better than humans. But what might their hearing mechanism be?

Carl Gancher, fellow in creativity and consciousness at University of Southern Califragilistic, believes Blue Man Group's entire body may act as a sensory receptor, allowing them the ability to absorb extrasensory data about the world around them. He explains, "The human ear is a transducer①—it converts one type of energy into another. Take the eardrum②, it vibrates in response to pressure waves created by sounds. It is possible the entire Blue Man body works the same way."

Many have attempted to re-create the full-body transducer experience, but it remains a distinguished difference between Blue Man and human.

①Other examples of transducers include microphones, antennas, and evil sorcerers. ②Although very small, the eardrum is an actual drum.

BLUE MAN SENSES: TOUCH

ASIDE FROM ITS HUE, the major observable difference between human skin and Blue Man skin is the rapidity with which Blue Man skin regenerates. Because of this lightning-fast growth, their skin is in a constant state of fluidity and as a consequence leaves itself on every surface and object that the Blue Men come into direct physical contact with. A unique feature of this transferred skin is that it remains fluid and appears to survive separation for long periods of time.

This fact might suggest that Blue Man Group's sense of touch is extended beyond their physical bodies. That perhaps the traces of skin left behind on people and objects continually transmit sensations back to the Blue Men of origin. In this way, it is possible that the Blue Men retain a connection to the things they touch long after the happening is over.

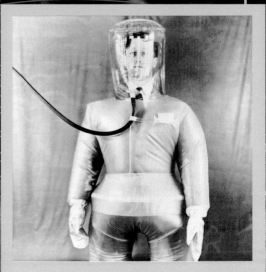

This photograph suggests there are many who will go to extreme measures to avoid the connection created by touch.

An interesting but less universally accepted theory comes from Soviet biologist Алекса́ндр Ива́нович Опа́рин (aka Alexander Ivanovich Oparin) and the groundbreaking research in his book *The Origination of Life*. He contends that Blue Man Group's skin is comprised of primordial ooze.

BLUE MAN SENSES: TASTE/SMELL

TOBLERONE

JELLO | PAINT

CEREAL | TWINKIE

MARSHMALLOW

SCIENTIFIC EVIDENCE regarding Blue Man Group's sense of taste is virtually nonexistent. Already one of the more subjective senses to test, we are left to interpret what we can from Blue Man Group's behavior.

According to rheologist Dr. Fran Bailey, "I think it's too big a leap to even assume the Blue Men consume food the way we do. Food may not be their sustenance at all. It's possible they survive on far different or far greater things than what we call 'nutrients.'"

QUAKER

CAP'N CRUNCH

Love that Crunch!

When asked about Blue Man Group's ability to receive pleasure from tasting food, art historian and Warhol enthusiast Josie Kirkadilly responded, "I believe when the Blue Men consume or explore food, they are hungry for information about our culture and how we mass produce, market and consume food products, including the edible ones."

It is likely the Blue Men
are drawn to food
not by its nutritional value,
but by its malleability,
viscosity, packaging,
musicality, and
projectile potential.

Regarding smell,
the Blue Men have no
discernible olfactory
system at all. No one
has ever observed them
smelling anything.

CAP'N
RUNC

CAP'N
RUNCH

It is unclear whether the scientific
experiment taking place in this
photograph has anything to do
with the exploration of Blue Man
Group's ability to taste or smell.

BLUE MAN SENSES:
SYNESTHESIA

IF THE BLUE MEN SEE, smell, hear, taste, and feel the world differently than humans, one reason might be that they possess a kind of synesthetic ability that enhances their perceptual experience.

Synesthesia is a neurological phenomenon in which stimulation of one sensory or cognitive pathway leads to automatic, involuntary experience in a second sensory or cognitive pathway.

For example, the ability to see sound, to taste music, to feel color, to hear food, to smell art.

To illustrate this, here are a few forms of synesthesia.

BP1
BP2

VISUAL-TACTILE
SYNESTHESIA

3.3V
10K   POT1

G1
R1

AH

H6

G2
G3

3.3V
10K   POT1

V_M3
V_M2
V_M1

VISUAL-TACTILE SYNESTHESIA
When the sight of something triggers the sense of touch or a physical sensation in the body.

Robert Lillie, visual perception expert and Midwest regional manager at LensCrafters says, "I am of the belief that some of Blue Man Group's rituals are an attempt to change our perception and transform our ability to see. It's as if they want us to experience synesthesia. The implication is that these colors and lights were always there, but through the process of this ritual we're now able to see them①."

CHROMESTHESIA

CHROMESTHESIA
When sounds and musical
tones trigger seeing colors.

LEXICAL-
GUSTATORY
SYNESTHESIA

LEXICAL-GUSTATORY
SYNESTHESIA
When words trigger
the sensation of taste.

SECTION

1

47

SLEEP MORNING
LOST SWIMMING FLY DREAM BRIDGE
FREEDOM FLOAT COLD BUBBLE PEOPLE
SEE LOVE ART BLUE HEART
GROW BLACK DIRECTION WATER SKY COLOR OCEAN YOUNG
CALL VISION SKY NOISE GLASS
HOME RED ORANGE WINDOW GRASS MOTHER PURPLE SOUND NO
PILLOW HOUSE MOTION YES SOUND
PLAY YES FIRE

The Morton Heilig Sensorama
machine invented in 1957
promised to deliver a
multi-sensory experience to
its audiences.

① See Collective Synesthesia, page 174.

MODALITY THEORY

GROUP
MEMBER

EXPERT OPINION regarding Blue Man behavior falls into three distinct theories:

Dr. Irving Bock:
THE MODALITY THEORY
Dr. Errol Farber-Harbin:
**THE TRIPARTITE SIPHONOPHORIC THEORY
(OR THREE-AS-ONE THEORY)**
Dr. Anna Boyd:
THE ID/SUPEREGO THEORY

THE MODALITY THEORY
Dr. Irving Bock, professor of post-semantic philosophy at New Hampshire Institute of Non-Applicable Psychology, has constructed a chart based on his decades of research on Blue Man behavior.[1] "This chart displays the six primary modalities into which all observable Blue Man behavior can be categorized. The Blue Men seem to have the ability to move nimbly from one mind-set to another. Perhaps most remarkable is their ability to exhibit characteristics of opposite dualities at the same time. This is one of the things that makes their behavior so mysterious and charismatic."

INNOCENT

"The behavior of the Blue Men is completely dy-
namic one moment to another. They move fluidly
through the modalities. If you look closely, my chart
illustrates how, if you move too far into 'Hero mode'
for example, you lose your 'Innocent,' and so on.
The more you are of one, the less you are of its
opposite. What's remarkable about the Blue Men is
that they seem to have the ability to inhabit a space
in the center of the circle where they have a connection to all six mind-sets." —Dr. Irving Bock

SCIENTIST

HERO

SHAMAN

TRICKSTER

THE FIRST PAIR OF OPPOSING MIND-SETS IN BOCK'S CHART IS THE SCIENTIST AND THE SHAMAN.

Dr. Bock describes the Scientist as someone who "accumulates facts about the outside world, constructs hypotheses, and then attempts to prove them. The Scientist observes, deduces, unpacks, predicts, tests, questions, demonstrates, and validates. The Scientist is logical, methodical, consistent, objective, and rational."

BLUE MAN BEHAVIOR:
SCIENTIST/ SHAMAN

FAMOUS SCIENTISTS: Albert Einstein, Stephen Hawking, Jane Goodall, Neil deGrasse Tyson, Marie Curie, Carl Sagan, Sir Isaac Newton, Nikola Tesla, Ben Franklin, Carl Linnaeus, Leonardo da Vinci, Alexander Graham Bell, Hermann Rorschach

FAMOUS SHAMANS: David Bowie, Maya Angelou, Mark Rothko, Kramer, Jim Morrison, Obi-Wan Kenobi, Gandalf, Merlin, Marie Laveau, Nikola Tesla, Oprah Winfrey, Mother Teresa, Tim Burton, Karen Finley, Krishna, Willem de Kooning, Yves Klein, Bob Dylan, Elvis Presley Joseph Campbell, John Coltrane, Jimi Hendrix, Frida Kahlo, Janis Joplin, Prince, George Clinton

A "shaman" is commonly regarded as "a person having access to, and influence in, the world of spirits." The field of Blue Man studies, however, defines "Shaman" somewhat differently. According to Bock, "The Shaman is about the subjective inner world of the imagination. The Shaman is primal and instinctual rather than intellectual and lives in a world of music, mystery, and creative expression. At times the Shaman can be a trance[1],[2] inducer or a ritual leader and their work often inspires others to become more creative.

[1] Trance: from the Old French *transir*, "to depart," and from the Latin *transire*, "go across." Trance states are fundamentally about traversing the distance between our everyday reality and another plane of existence.
[2] The Blue Men also appear interested in elements of contemporary trance music or rave culture, such as translucent clothing, dancing, fractals, altered states of consciousness, big crazy parties, and sugary childhood snacks. They have not yet been observed wearing raver pants, plastic beads, candy necklaces, lollipops, or rolling around on the floor giggling, then puking, then crying, then giggling.

BLUE MAN
BEHAVIOR:
HERO/INNOCENT

52

**THE SECOND PAIR OF OPPOSING MODALITIES
IN THE MODEL IS HERO AND INNOCENT.**

The "Hero energy," in the words of Dr. Bock, is goal oriented and
"can best be described as one moving forward in spite of chal-
lenges, difficulties or risks." In this modality, the focus is on the
objective and how to stoically achieve it at all costs.

The Innocent, on the other hand, lives entirely in the moment and with no outward goal. Rather than being hardened for battle, the innocent is emotionally exposed and vulnerable. In the stillness of this gentle presence the Innocent can harness the power of surrender and the wisdom of authenticity.

FAMOUS HEROES: Joan of Arc, Bilbo Baggins, Henry V, firefighters, Neo, Trinity, Nelson Mandela, Desmond Tutu, Malala Yousafzai, Jonas Salk, Bruce Lee, Muhammad Ali, Amelia Earhart, Florence Nightingale, Odysseus, Sinbad, Jason (the Argonaut), half of Tom Hanks's roles

Less frequently recognized but equally important heroes include the IT guy, single parents, and fifth-grade math teachers.

FAMOUS INNOCENTS: Forrest Gump, Amélie, Andy Kaufman's Latka in *Taxi*, Charlie Chaplin, Goofy, Winnie-the-Pooh, Buster Keaton, Chauncey Gardner, Harpo, the other half of Tom Hanks's roles

THE FINAL PAIR OF OPPOSING MIND-SETS IN BOCK'S CHART IS GROUP MEMBER AND TRICKSTER.

The Group Member mind-set is about establishing and maintaining group cohesion. Group Members put their energy toward helping organizations collaborate at a high level of complexity and alignment. According to Bock, the Group Member puts the need of the collective above the needs of the self. Moreover Group Members tend to the structures required for groups to run smoothly.

BLUE MAN BEHAVIOR:
GROUP MEMBER/ TRICKSTER

FAMOUS GROUP MEMBERS: ducks, marching bands, synchronized swimmers, flying trapeze acts, a flock of seagulls,[1] symphony orchestras, offensive lines, 1980 Team USA Men's Olympic Hockey Team, and HR professionals

FAMOUS TRICKSTERS: Loki, Andy Kaufman, Groucho Marx, Lenny Bruce, Richard Pryor, Mel Brooks, Monty Python, Kristen Wiig, Fred Armisen, Harlequin, Jackie Chan, Johnny Knoxville, Keith Moon, Sarah Silverman, Charlie Chaplin, Captain Jack Sparrow, Louis C. K., Bugs Bunny, Sid Vicious, Ricky Gervais, Carol Burnett, George Clinton

The Trickster is all about breaking rules and striking out on one's own. The Trickster is a maverick who is weary of the stultifying effects of bureaucratic red tape. Whether it is the jester who makes fun of the king, the punk rocker who mocks the establishment, or the inventor who swings out into unexplored territory, the Trickster crosses boundaries, takes chances, and is willing to break social norms and go it alone.

① Not to be confused with the band, A Flock of Seagulls.

TRIPARTITE SIPHONOPHORIC THEORY

Farber-Harbin's theory grows out of his time studying endosymbiosis, the evolutionary process by which smaller organisms join forces, living in symbiosis inside greater organisms. Our own cells are products of endosymbiosis; the mitochondria that generate chemical energy for our cells are actually descended from bacteria that began living inside larger cells. Each of our cells is a community of life-forms.[5]

Like our own cells, the Blue Men appear to be separate individuals. However, they are so profoundly connected that they function as a single organism.[6]

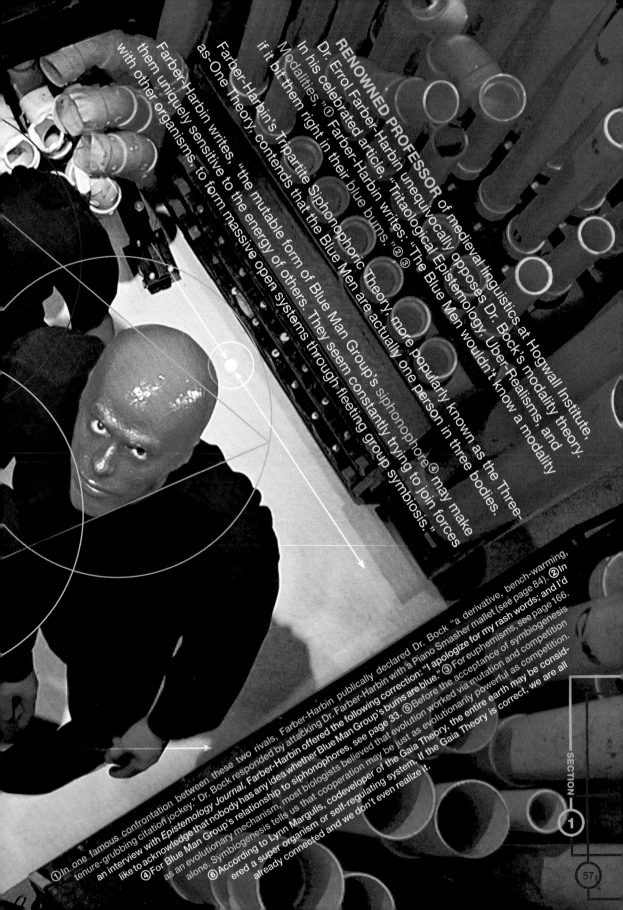

RENOWNED PROFESSOR of medieval linguistics at Hogwall Institute, Dr. Errol Farber-Harbin unequivocally opposes Dr. Bock's modality theory. In his celebrated article, "Tritadological Epistemology, Uber-Realisms, and Modalities,"[1] Farber-Harbin writes: "The Blue Men wouldn't know a modality if it bit them right in their blue bums."[2][3]

Farber-Harbin writes, "the mutable form of Blue Man Group's siphonophoric[4] may make them uniquely sensitive to the energy of others. They seem constantly trying to join forces with other organisms, to form massive open systems through fleeting group symbiosis."

Farber-Harbin's Tripartite Siphonophoric Theory, more popularly known as the Three-as-One Theory, contends that the Blue Men are actually one person in three bodies.

[1] In one famous confrontation between these two rivals, Farber-Harbin publically declared Dr. Bock "a derivative, bench-warming, tenure-grubbing citation jockey." Dr. Bock responded by attacking Dr. Farber-Harbin with a Piano Smasher mallet (see page 84). [2] In an interview with *Epistemology Journal,* Farber-Harbin offered the following correction: "I apologize for my rash words, and I'd like to acknowledge that nobody has any idea whether Blue Man Group's bums are blue." [3] For euphemisms, see page 166. [4] For Blue Man Group's relationship to siphonophores, see page 33. [5] Before the acceptance of symbiogenesis as an evolutionary mechanism, most biologists believed that evolution worked via mutation and competition alone. Symbiogenesis tells us that cooperation may be just as evolutionarily powerful as competition. [6] According to Lynn Margulis, codeveloper of the Gaia Theory, the entire earth may be considered a super organism or self-regulating system. If the Gaia Theory is correct, we are all already connected and we don't even realize it.

BLUE MAN BEHAVIOR:
ID/SUPEREGO THEORY, AKA FREUDIAN THEORY

Dr. David Lindquist, Child Therapist in Laguna Beach, California, speculates, "The Blue Man is not alien, yet not human. But he does touch our human history. Perhaps the Blue Man reminds us of who we want to be, what we might have lost and what we could become."

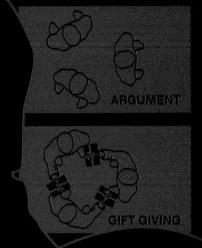

MEETING

ARGUMENT

GIFT GIVING

THE FINAL, and perhaps most often challenged, behavioral theory is attributed to Dr. Anne Boyd of Gronehaben University in Rotterdam. Dr. Boyd has postulated a classification of Blue Man behavior based on the work of Dr. Sigmund Freud, specifically his analytical breakdown of the human psyche into:

ID: Defined by Freud as human instinct; pure innocence with no history, no neuroses, living fully in the moment.

SUPEREGO: The moral conscience, the drive to do the right thing, to ignore fear, and follow a higher path no matter what the cost.

EGO: One's outward personality, the artifice that one presents to the world around them, the mask that people create to protect themselves and help them "fit in."

"It is my belief," says Dr. Boyd, "that the Blue Men are themselves completely devoid of the ego and live in constant movement between the id and the superego. They represent the 'removal' of the mask and a life of honesty, free from pretense." [1]

[1] For more on masks, see page 138.

SECTION—1

WHILE THE SCOPE AND SCALE of the various Blue Man behavioral studies may vary greatly, they all share a common belief—that the Blue Men are hardwired to desire and create connectedness.[1] First and foremost, they connect with each other, then the ritual participants, and finally with the world at large.

CONNECT WITH EACH OTHER

WORLD AT LARGE

BLUE MAN
BEHAVIOR:
CONNECTEDNESS

CRAZY   SEXY   COOL

FAMOUS TRIOS: *My Three Sons;*
The Three Musketeers; the Three
Stooges; "The Three Blind Mice";
Nirvana; Kim, Kourtney, and
Khloe; *Josie and the Pussycats;*
The Good, the Bad & the Ugly;
Destiny's Child; TLC; BLT;
DMV; Snap, Crackle, and
Pop; the tri-state area;
the Marx Brothers[2]

RITUAL
PARTICIPANTS

SECTION

①

61

[1] Perhaps this is a note of particular distinction in our culture, where
we are increasingly focused on (some would say obsessed with) the
individual, as opposed to the group. **[2] Except for Zeppo.**

SECTION 2
THE BLUE MAN
WORLD

THE NEXT STEP IN UNDERSTANDING THE BLUE MAN WORLD IS TO EXAMINE THE FUNDAMENTAL ELEMENTS OF THEIR RITUALISTIC HAPPENINGS.

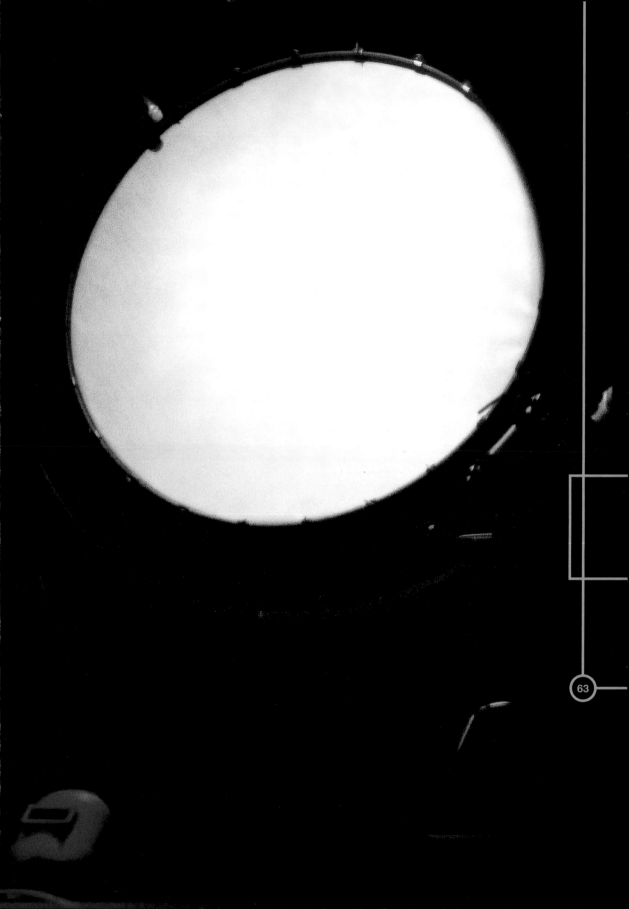

SUBLIME SPACES

THE BLUE MEN APPEAR TO BE attracted to sublime and extraordinary spaces. They may choose to occupy a theater, a rooftop, a basement, a yurt, a sanctuary, a subway ca a butte, a desert, or a mountaintop.

YOU'RE
ALL
WASTED

Some experts assert that while the Blue Men may be drawn to rarified spaces, a public assemblage must be present in order for a ritual to take place. According to cultural anthropologist Marcy McCormack, "The desire to congregate in groups and participate in primal rituals is something innate, and hard wired into our DNA. This feature of humans probably evolved over hundreds of thousands of years of tribal life and will stay in our DNA no matter how 'modern' we become."[1]

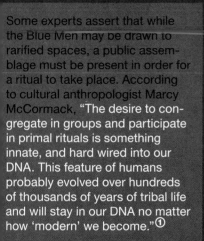

[1] How else could one explain the endurance of live events such as theater, rock and roll, sporting matches, and *Star Trek* conventions?

INTRINSIC
ELEMENTS

MUSICAL INSTRUMENTS

MUSIC APPEARS TO be almost omnipresent in the Blue Man world. Ethnomusicologist Morris Cheeba provides a helpful overview of the significance of music to the Blue Man experience: "Music sets the tone, creates the mood, and guides the listeners through the journey. Some believe the Blue Men simply cannot generate a collective gestalt without music. Others are more inclined to believe music is literally the language of the Blue Men. But the simplest explanation, and my personal belief, is that the Blue Men simply love to rock."

DRUMBONE

FATTIE
FATTIE
SKINNIES
SKINNIES

69

.32   .20   .1◯   *
.22   .18   .14   *.22

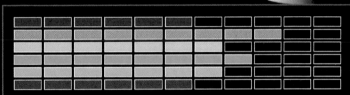

The Blue Men play music on one-of-a-kind instruments, often constructed out of unexpected materials. From Paint Drums and PVC to more uncommon objects like logs, smoke, or even food, the materials they use to make music can often appear random. However, according to Cheeba, "upon closer inspection, it is clear the Blue Men prioritize certain characteristics when choosing their instruments. I've outlined those characteristics below and ranked these characteristics as they pertain to each instrument on a scale that goes to eleven."

AT ONCE MODERN AND ANCIENT
Degree to which an instrument communicates a simultaneously primeval and contemporary aesthetic.

TRANSMOGRIFICATION
Extent to which an object has been transformed from its original state into a functional instrument.

MOBILITY
Extent to which the instrument can rock while it rolls.

SYNESTHESIA
Degree to which the instrument demonstrates a metaphoric crossing of the senses.

KICKASSOMETRY
Total amount of butt the instrument kicks.

LUMINOSITY
Amount of glow or life force expressed by the instrument.

THE PVC IS ARGUABLY[1] the most recognizable of all Blue Man instruments. It is a mammoth structure made of polyvinyl chloride plumbing pipe that varies in diameter. The Blue Men transform this modern material, typically used by human populations to transport potable water and nonpotable waste, into a melodic percussive instrument. Blue Man Group's rhythmic drumming forces air through the tubes, while the length of the pipe determines the pitch of the note.

In 2003, Blue Man Group stunned the music world with their cover of Donna Summer's "I Feel Love"[2],[3] by replicating Giorgio Moroder's[4] entirely synthesized electronic bass line on the purely acoustic and physically played PVC instrument. Noted ethnomusicologist and chaos theoretician, Dr. Malcolm Gladhand marvels, "They are an analog anomaly in an increasingly electronic world."

In the ultimate Blue Man *vs.* Machine, the trio also reproduced, note for note, the entirely automated synthesizer opener to The Who's "Baba O'Riley."[5]

INSTRUMENTS:
THE PVC

AT ONCE MODERN & ANCIENT
TRANSMOGRIFY
MOBILITY
SYNESTHESIA
KICKASSOMETRY
LUMINOSITY

There are pros and cons to working with PVC. Pro: Once assembled, it only needs to be tuned every ten to fifteen thousand years. Con: Once assembled, the instrument can only be taken apart by sawing it into pieces with the use of commercial-grade cutting tools normally available only to the plumbing trade.

The Blue Men seem to have their own color-based, non-chromatic musical system that values not only the music, but also the theatricality and physicality with which it is played. Each note corresponds to a color rather than a letter.

SECTION 2

71

① Many experts disagree with the use of the word "arguably" in this context, contending that "conceivably" or "perhaps" would be more precise. ② "I Feel Love" by Donna Summer is a disco* song, heavily reliant on electric synthesized beats. ③ In their article "How Donna Summer's 'I Feel Love' Changed Pop" published in 2012 in *The Guardian,* Jon Savage and Ewan Pearson wrote of the song: "Within its modulations and pulses it achieves the perfect state of grace that is the ambition of every dance record: it obliterates the tyranny of the clock—the everyday world of work, responsibility, money—and creates its own time, a moment of pleasure, ecstasy and motion that seems infinitely expandable, if not eternal." ④ Depending on how you feel about disco music, Giorgio Moroder can either be praised or blamed for its popularity. Either way, his prolific career is pretty impressive. ⑤ It is believed that Pete Townshend recorded the opener to "Baba O'Riley" using a Lowrey Berkshire Deluxe TBO-1 organ with its "marimba" feature as a backing track. *In this instance, "disco" refers to heavily synthesized dance music, rather than the unincorporated community in Blount County, Tennessee.

INSTRUMENTS: BACKPACK TUBULUM

WHILE THE PVC MAY BE the most widely recognized Blue Man instrument, its usefulness is severely limited due to its size and weight. Presumably the Backpack Tubulum was invented to compensate for this deficiency.

The Backpack Tubulum is constructed of larger-diameter PVC pipes, mounted to a hiking pack frame, which allows the Blue Men to strap it onto their backs. Once secured, the Blue Men are free to roam about, facilitating more intimate contact with those around them.

AT ONCE MODERN & ANCIENT
TRANSMOGRIFY
MOBILITY
SYNESTHESIA
KICKASSOMETRY

THOUGH THE ORIGIN of the name "Drumbone" is unknown, it is believed this portmanteau① refers to the percussive nature of a drum combined with the telescoping slide mechanism of a trombone, which is used to control the instrument's pitch.

The Drumbone is made of drain, waste, and vent standard-wall PVC pipes, which slide in and out of larger cardboard tubes.

Possibly the most notable feature of this instrument is that it requires the three Blue Men working in unison to accomplish an entire melody. Thus, the Drumbone is a prime example of gestalt,② in which each individual must make a distinct contribution to the whole in order to achieve something greater than the individual elements.

INSTRUMENTS: DRUMBONE

AT ONCE MODERN & ANCIENT
TRANSMOGRIFY
MOBILITY
STREAMLINE
KICKASSOMETER
LUMINOSITY

75

Dr. Errol Farber-Harbin cites the playing of the Drumbone as evidence for his Tripartite Siphonophoric Theory (or as it is more popularly known, the Three-as-One Theory). Here, the Blue Men are clearly separate individuals, but they are so profoundly connected that they function as a single organism in order to complete the task at hand.[3]

Others note this is the same type of extreme teamwork required by competitive Double Dutchers.

[1] For more information on portmanteaus, see page 146. [2] For the definition of "gestalt," see page 161. [3] For more on Dr. Farber-Harbin's theory, see page 56.

INSTRUMENTS: DRUMS

DRUMS CAN BE FOUND in nearly every civilization since the dawn of time. Though the styles may vary from groups such as the Kodo drummers[1] to Keith Moon[2] to djembe jam sessions[3] to Brazilian baterias[4] all cultures seem to share the primal urge to create tribal rhythms. The Blue Men are no different in this regard.

Morris Cheeba confirms, "There is nothing surprising about the Blue Men choosing drums as the core of their communication. Drums speak directly to our primal selves. What is remarkable is the way in which the Blue Men use them, with such power and veracity that the vibrations and sound waves literally shake our chest cavities. They rattle us into remembering where we come from."

Evidence of the Blue Men playing various styles of drumming in various cultures exists.

BRAZILIAN BATERIAS

KODO DRUMMERS

NYC STREET DRUMMING

①Incredible drummers from Japan. ②Keith Moon* was the legendary drummer for The Who and a gonzo rock personality. ③A djembe is a powerful drum from West Africa. ④A Brazilian Carnival term for the drum section of a samba band. This section provides the rhythm for the parade.† *Known as "Moon the Loon" by friends. Also, the inspiration for Dr. Teeth and The Electric Mayhem's‡ drummer, Animal. †Artur da Távola (1936–2008), Brazilian writer and poet said, "The rhythm is definitely the most primitive of our sensorial experiences. Thus, it follows us through our lives and it stands for the basic assumption of vitality, since when it's over, life has ended." ‡*The Muppet Show* band.

INSTRUMENTS:
PAINT DRUMS

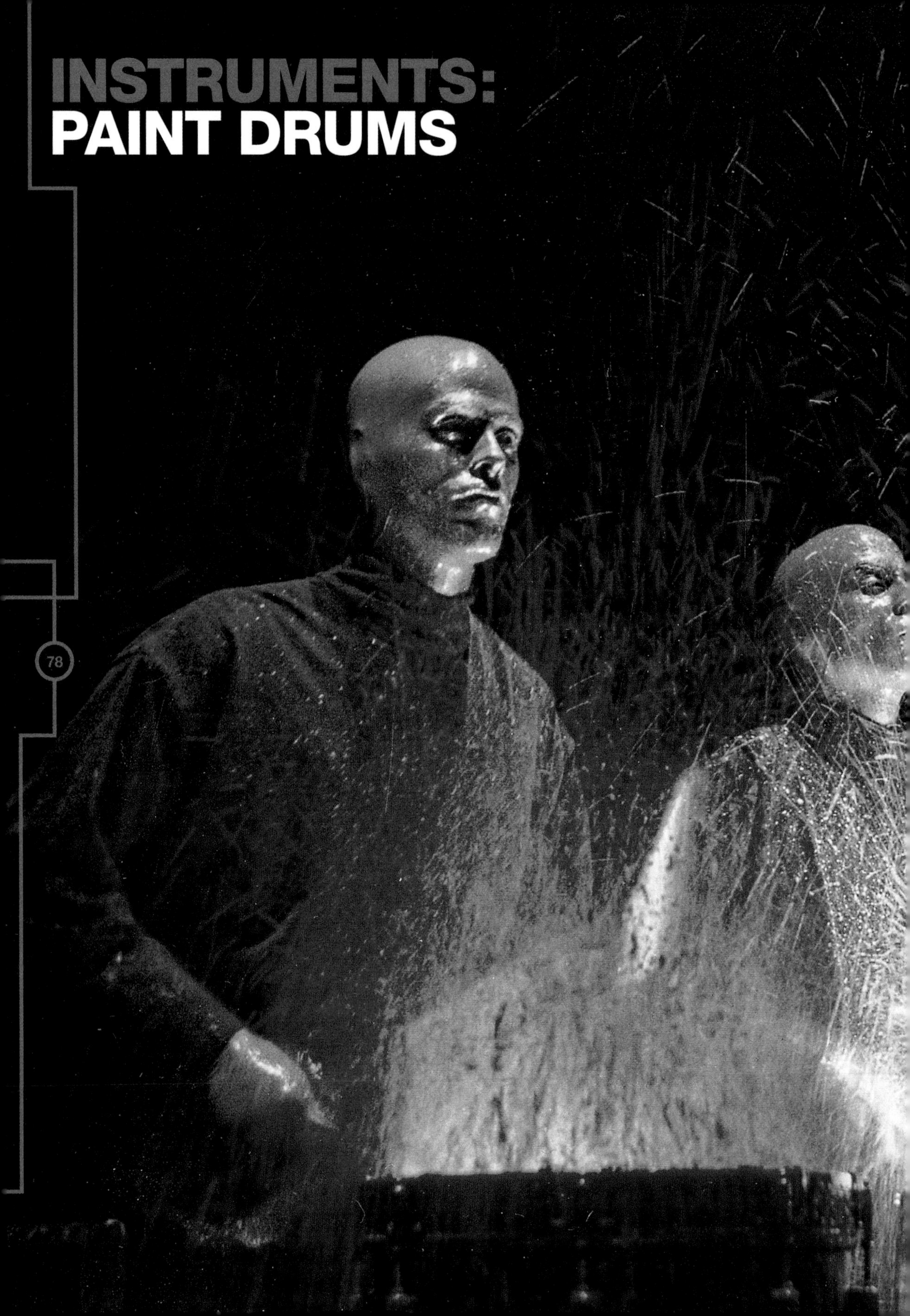

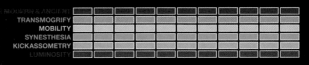

AT ONCE MODERN & ANCIENT									
TRANSMOGRIFY									
MOBILITY									
SYNESTHESIA									
KICKASSOMETRY									
LUMINOSITY									

The Paint Drums exceed all the metrics of Cheeba's measurement tool. The only other known instrument to come anywhere close to this belongs to esteemed composer Nigel Tufnel.

PERHAPS THE MOST VISUALLY STUNNING and emotionally expressive instrument in the Blue Man world are the Paint Drums.

When the Blue Men play a set of Paint Drums, their powerful drumbeats are accompanied by explosive glowing liquid. It is believed they are attempting to create a synesthesia-like experience by merging powerful movement, tribal sounds, and luminescent color. The drumbeats are rendered visible[1] to the human eye as the paint, the light, and the sound waves explode into one entity.

SECTION 2

79

[1] Many Blue Man devotees are also interested in the effect of percussion on matter. For a good time, find an online video of non-Newtonian liquids on a speaker cone.

SMOKE DRUMS

WHEN STRUCK WITH SUFFICIENT FORCE, Smoke Drums produce a giant ring of smoke, or, as scientists call them, billowing toroidal① vortices②.

It has been suggested that the inspiration for this instrument was the enormous billboard that, for years, blew smoke rings over Time Square.

Others believe the Blue Men were inspired by a more natural source—Italy's Mount Etna volcano, which occasionally puffs smoke rings into Sicily's perfect blue skies.

①From the word "toroid," a fancy way of saying "doughnut shape." ②A toroidal vortex (also called a "vortex ring"), involves a flow pattern in a toroidal shape wherein rotating fluid moves through the same or different fluid. The movement of the fluid is on the circular axis of the ring, in a twisting vortex motion.

INSTRUMENTS: MOBILE BIOMORPHIC UNITS

IN RECENT TIMES, the Blue Men appear to have drawn from nature to take their biomorphic mobile instruments to the next level.

THE PHOENIX appears to be an anthropomorphic mechanized ambulatory sculpture. It has six "arms" with drums and log drums attached to the ends. These arms move individually from a range directly in front of the Blue Man to a seemingly impossible spread of nine feet. This movement resembles the spreading wings of the Phoenix from Greek mythology.

THE SPIDER is often seen in tandem with the Phoenix. It is a similar moving drum sculpture with numerous drums mounted on it. Its pneumatic legs resemble the legs of a spider. It also has the optional Snarepion[1] mounted on the rear. In order to employ the Snarepion, the Blue Man pulls an overhead lever actuating a mechanical array of numerous drumsticks that strike five different snare drums in a stinging drum flam.

THE PERCUSSIPEDES are sleek and sculptural in nature, like a flowing steel skeleton of a futuristic prehistoric beastie. Each one has a unique assortment of drums and percussion mounted on it for the Blue Men to pummel while pulling the peripatetic beast of batterie along a desired route. Illuminated spider legs crawl along with the movement.

AT ONCE MODERN & ANCIENT
TRANSMOGRIFY
MOBILITY
SYNESTHESIA
KICKASSOMETRY
LUMINOSITY

It is not uncommon for scientists to use inspiration from nature (biomimicry) to solve a human problem.

VELCRO was inspired by how plant burrs stick to animal hair.

E-READER SCREENS that reflect light (rather than transmit light) are inspired by the way in which butterfly wings glow in bright light.

COOLING DEVICES are being developed based on the way the fogstand beetle of the Namib Desert collects water by condensing fog into droplets on the ridges of its back.

83

①Snarepion: Like a scorpion but with a snare.

STRINGED
PIECES

AT ONCE MODERN & ANCIENT

TRANSMOGRIFY
MOBILITY
SYNESTHESIA
KICKASSOMETRY
LUMINOSITY

PIANO SMASHER

...aby grand piano is deconstructed. The high
...gs are removed and replaced by additional low
...gs, then tuned to a single note or progression
...ur notes at most. When struck by a large
...let, the result is a tonal thunderclap of bone-
...nching reverberation.

THE BLUE MEN
have also
been known to
employ string
instruments.
However, in
almost all
cases these
instruments
are used in
a percussive
fashion.

HUNGARIAN CIMBALOM

is a type of hammered dulcimer consisting of a trapezoidal box with metal strings stretched across the top. Normally the instrument is played by hitting the strings with short, padded sticks called beaters. The Blue Men, however, utilize heavy, wooden drum sticks with shaved ends. This provides more of an "attack," which gives it an edgier sound than originally intended.

AT ONCE MODERN & ANCIENT
TRANSMOGRIFY
MOBILITY
SYNESTHESIA
KICKASSOMETRY
LUMINOSITY

SPINULUM

The Spinulum looks like a vertical banjo but sounds like an alien humming. Nameless after its conception and realization, it was referred to for months as "The Spinny Thing" or by simply making a turning or winding motion with one's hand. It works by running small bits of rigid plastic, attached to a circular, hand-spun wheel, across two piano strings. Pitch is controlled by a sliding mechanism along the "neck."

AT ONCE MODERN & ANCIENT
TRANSMOGRIFY
MOBILITY
SYNESTHESIA
KICKASSOMETRY
LUMINOSITY

ALL OTHER INSTRUMENTS

AIRPOLE A long boat antenna that makes a percussive "whoosh" as it slices through the air. Easy to play, dangerous to stand next to.①

THE BIG DRUM Five feet in diameter, this drum creates a low, frequency sonic boom when struck with a big honking mallet.②

BRAIN DRUM A massive—bigger than the Big Drum—fiberglass drum, played with huge hammers and filled with LEDs. Its shape resembles a synapse rather than a whole brain, but "Synaptic Drum" doesn't scan quite as well.

CHIMEULUM A giant set of midi-enhanced steel③ pipes hung from a truss and played with a wooden mallet.

CIMBALOM Adapted from the Hungarian cimbalom, but with more strings, this large dulcimer is played with modified drumsticks. Visually, it resembles an open-faced piano sandwich.④

The Big Drum

DRUMULUM A four-inch diameter PVC pipe of relatively long length—and hence low pitch—mounted over a large floor tom. When the drum head is struck, it sends a deep tone through the opening. Works like a human eardrum, sounds like a sweet synthesizer. See also *Slideulum*.

EBOW 1. A type of alternative, electric bow for people trying to quit the violin. 2. A bow implanted with battery-operated electromagnetic pulses, so that the string vibrates rapidly.

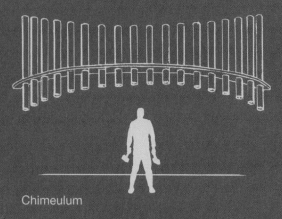

Chimeulum

GARY BALLS Stainless steel spherical tank floats with slits cut into them, suspended by thin bungee cords. When struck with mallets, they emit a pitched but microtonal percussive sound.

GARY STRIPS These long, flat aluminum sheets create a thunderous, high-frequency alternative to snare drums.

GYRO SHOT Spinning, circular rings filled with ball bearings of varying sizes.[5]

HUGE DRUMSTICK
A giant drumstick.[6]

LOGULUM Exactly what it sounds like: a collection of one-note wooden drums tangentially related to the Hawaiian slit drum, combined to create one massive percussion instrument. It's almost an onomatopoeia.

PVC Busstopulum

MAMBLER This giant mechanized contraption housed many drums, an enormous video screen, a tail that could act as a birth canal, and an instrument called the Whack-a-Moleulum, among other eclectic features.[7]

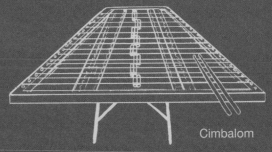

Cimbalom

Drumulum

MANDELDRUMS A set of Paint Drums enhanced with multiple LED panels displaying messages. Named after Benoit Mandelbrot, who introduced the world to the fractal-generating mathematical equation known as the "Mandelbrot set".[8]

ORBS These little glass balls light up when they are hit.

①Some speculate that this instrument was inspired by the common saying "you could put an eye out." ②A relic of a time when giant drums roamed the earth, before they were all eaten by prehistoric man. Most Big Drums died out around the year 5000 BCE, but a handful survive in a few extreme environments. ③"Midi" refers to Musical Instrument Digital Interface ④Also the electric cimbalom, a powered version of the same played with heavy drumsticks for a more aggressive sound. ⑤Although it looks really cool and industrial, the truth is the Gyro Shot sounds like a wimpy rain stick. As a result, this instrument does not appear anywhere in rituals or recordings. ⑥A mallet, if you want to get technical about it. ⑦The Mambler is currently enjoying retirement. ⑧The association is obvious, isn't it?

ALL OTHER INSTRUMENTS

ROCKET TOMS Vertically mounted small drums tuned to definite pitches that the Blue Men play during the song referred to as "Klein." Also known as Doppler drums.

PHIL DRUMS Vertically mounted big drums tuned much lower that accompany the Rocket Toms.

PIPEULUM An array of slit iron pipes. A heavy-duty hose with an industrial nozzle is used to blast hot steam into the pipes, creating a low, airy tone.

Pipeulum

POWER CHORDULUM A stringed instrument meant to be played gently, but with a hammer.[9]

QUELLEULUM No one knows what this is, but it is believed to exist.

SABERBONE Like a Drumbone, but bigger, lower-pitched, and frankly a bit more intimidating.

SHAKER GONG A metal-encased matrix of ball bearings that is suspended from tightly stretched surgical tubing. When hit with a large, padded mallet, it produces a sustained, metallic, rattlesnake-like sound.

SHAKERS LED signs with a shaker attached to them.

DOGULUM
No one has ever seen this mysterious instrument but it is believed to be a xylophone made out of dogs of various sizes that bark a certain tone when patted gently or scratched behind the ears.

SLIDEULUM A Drumulum with a Drumbone-like slide attachment, which allows the pitch to be varied while the drum is being played.

THE GREAT HOUSEULUM EXPERIMENT

After constructing a brick colonial house from the ground up, the Blue Men chopped down a 140-foot Dutch Elm. The tree sliced the house in half, creating a decibel level of 140 dBA, making this "Houseulum" perhaps the largest percussion instrument on record. Logistical complications precluded the Blue Men from using the Houseulum in further rituals. It goes down in history as a sound heard once by few and remembered by many.

SNORKELBONE
Involves a plastic hose that—when swung in the air like a lasso—creates a whirring, pulsating tone. The pitch can be changed by a trombone-like mechanism that lengthens the hose. It fits like a snorkel in Blue Man Group's mouths. (The end of the hose, not the trombone-like mechanism.[10])

Snorkelbone

TONE SPOKES
Like a gigantic bicycle wheel with different length tubes as the spokes—it gets cranked around and is played with either a stick or another tube to create chords; sounds like a bassy drone.[11]

TUBULUM
The Tubulum is similar to the PVC instrument but has more of a twenty-first-century sound. It is struck with sticks rather than paddles and its notes are primarily in the bass range.

Tone Spokes

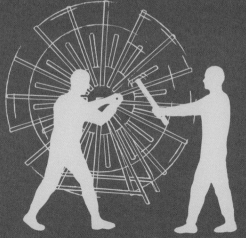

UTNE DRUM
Twenty-six-inch bass drum; hit with an LED sign. No drumsticks required.

VIDEO DRUM
Similar to Paint Drums—and modern versions of the Mandeldrums—almost like a GiPad inside clear acrylic drum shells. The video display responds to the playing of the drums.

[9] Imagine that Pete Townshend is stranded on a desert island with a cello and a sledgehammer. He might make a sound a lot like a Power Chordulum. [10] So it's a bagpipe trying to career pivot to become a bullroarer. [11] In action, the Tone Spokes looks like a Ferris wheel for midsized dogs.

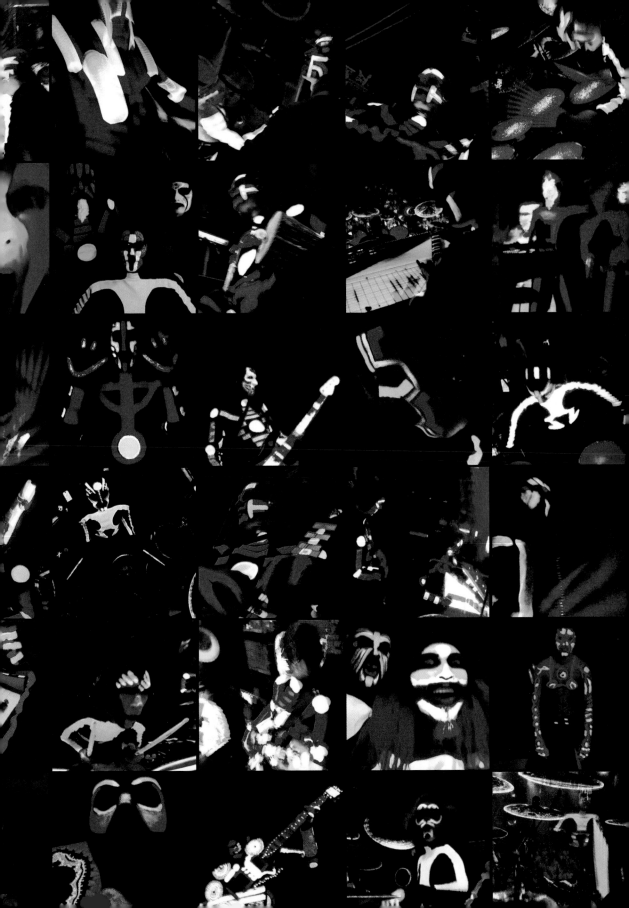

COLLABORATORS:
THE BAND

THROUGHOUT HISTORY,
certain individuals have claimed
to possess the ability to harness
the invisible wavelengths that bind
us all together. These individuals use
music or movement to lead others
into a trance-like state.

Some cultures call
these individuals **SHAMANS.**

Others call them
MONKS,
MEDICINE MEN,
DIVINERS,
ARTISTS,
or ## ROCK STARS.

In the world of
Blue Man Group, they are
THE BAND.[1]

93

① Not to be confused with the Canadian-American
rock group, the Band.

COLLABORATORS: THE BAND'S LOFTED SPACE

SURDO

A large floor tom eighteen, twenty, or twenty-two inches in diameter, it has a vinyl drumhead and is played with large mallets. Sometimes used in groups of three to create a melodic bass groove.

ICE BELL

A custom-made six-inch ice bell cymbal. Tuning is low and tribal.

TALKING DRUM

African instrument that was often used to communicate among tribes. Multiple strings run along the sides of its hourglass-shaped shell and serve to hold the two opposing drum skins on. The drum is held under one arm and squeezed to change the pitch. When hit with a mallet it makes "gulp" sounds. [6]

KIT

The Band's main percussive engine is a "standard" drum kit outfitted with extra toms and a dizzying array of cymbals and metal percussion. The result: a dense wall of pulsing percussion. Stand-up drum stations include percussion objects like ribbon crashers, Utne Drums, coil springs, cymbals, crashers, shakers, cowbell, the Brazilian timbau, the African ubu or talking drum, the metallic Spaceship, [4] and of course, more cowbell. [5]

FENDER JAZZMASTER GUITAR

A twangy electric guitar the sound of which recalls the reverb-laden spaghetti western soundtracks of Ennio Morricone [3]

CHAPMAN STICK

A ten-stringed guitar-bass hybrid developed in the 1950s by Emmett Chapman designed to be played by tapping fingers on the fretboard. In typical divergent fashion, The Band play only five of the strings using a bass string as a bow. Kind of like a grinding junkyard cello.[2]

TAMBORICA

Resembling a scorpion that lives behind the percussion player, the tamborica is a stack of eight six-inch drums with high-pitched drumheads. The many pairs of drumsticks are connected together with a cable system so all eight can be played at once.

BASS

Any band that likes to rock needs an electric bass, and Blue Man Group is no exception.[1]

ZITHER

The Band's principal stringed instrument, the zither has an upper harp-like section for melody lines and a lower multiple-chord section strung with guitar strings and meant to be played with a pick and slide. The zither lends itself to a wide range of techniques, however. The Pressaphonic, for example, involves banging the chord section with a metal tape measure.

EFFECTS PEDALS

[1] In Blue Man Group the bass is often subjected to so much processing during the live mix that it sounds unrecognizable—like an instrument in the witness protection program, or a bass that wishes to speak off the record. [2] Naturally, The Band mostly plays the two bottom notes by sawing strings with a length of heavy wound bass string. [3] Blue Man Group's guitars are equipped with whammy bars, which allow the player to express his or her inner whammy. [4] Also known as a hand pan or hang drum. The Band plays it with sticks and brushes instead of hands [5] Experts point to this aspect of ritual as evidence that the Blue Men are fans of prog rock. [6] Ever wonder what it sounds like when one of the Blue Men catches a marshmallow in his mouth? It's eerily similar to the sound of a talking drum…

COLLABORATORS:
THE BAND AND
THE BLUE MEN

BY ALL ACCOUNTS, members of The Band share a strong bond with the Blue Men. They appear to be highly attuned to the emotional state of the Blue Men and can react to the changing dynamics with great acuity.

COLLABORATORS:
THE C.R.E.W.

OF ALL THE COLLABORATORS IN THE BLUE MAN WORLD, none remain as mysterious and elusive as the shadowy beings that move about in the darkness. Referred to as the Courageous Resource of Exceptional Wisdom (or the C.R.E.W. for short), by all accounts, these hooded figures keep a watchful eye and are extremely capable at providing any necessary elements that the Blue Men might require. (See next page.)

There are rumors of a sacred preritual "crew gathering" that takes place between the Blue Men and all their collaborators. However no photographic evidence exists to support this claim.

LEAF BLOWERS, MUSIC DELIVERY SYSTEMS (BOOMBO
CANVAS, WELDING MASKS, CONSUMABLES, VARIOU
GUMBALL MACHINE, ROCK BOX, RECORDING DEVICE
IPADS, SHAVING CREAM, SHADOW PUPPETS, POLARO
MOUSETRAPS, PONCHOS, FUNNELATORS, VENTRILO
REMOTE CONTROLS, SHOWBOT, CATS, TOASTERS,
ELEPHANTS, BUNGEE CORDS, MONSTER TRUCKS, F
BLASTERS, ROLLS OF PAPER, CONFETTI, WHISTLES,
WITH PAINT, WATER GUNS (FILLED WITH PAINT), GI
LED SIGNS, FAKE PURSES, DEFIBRILLATORS, FLIP-FL
AND SCYTHES, ELECTRIC PENCIL SHARPENERS, CO
GAGA HAT, INFLATABLE BALL, POWDERED LAUNDRY
WELDING MASKS, FISHING POLES, PINK RUBBER SQUI
PETALS, AN ORNATE WOODEN BOX, ROAD CASES,
(À LA *CHARIOTS OF FIRE*), INDIANA JONES FEDORA
POWDERED WIGS AND GLOVES, BUCKETS OF PAINT,
BUTTONS, LICORICE, SCUBA MASKS, WATER WINGS,
TOWELS, FOLDING LAWN CHAIRS, BBQ GRILLS, BEAC
AIR DANCERS, WHOOPEE CUSHIONS, HAND BUZZE
DUCKIES, PEPPER GRINDERS, LEIS, COCONUT BRAS
SPORT, NOT THE HAIR), GOLD MEDALS, MARACAS, H
POWER DRILLS, CROWBARS, COLORFUL BAND-AIDS,
FLYSWATTERS, PRANK CANS OF SNAKES, ROTARY T
MUUMUUS, TREE COSTUMES, SELFIE STICKS, MINIA
BARS, VIKING HELMETS, WATER COOLERS FOOTBALL
PHONES, UPS GUYS, ANDREW WYETH'S *CHRISTINA'S*
DISCO BALLS, SAFETY GOGGLES, SUPER SOAKERS
OF BALL PIT BALLS, BUBBLE PIPES, OVERSIZED BLU
ANIMALS, BUG ZAPPERS, CLAPPER LIGHTS, HOLID
BAND LEADER HATS AND BATONS, VACUUMS, FEAT
ATMS, AWARD STATUETTES, RADIOS, CHOCOLATE M
MICS), ENVELOPES, BALLOONS, PLASTIC PROTECTIV
MOTORCYCLE HELMETS, PLASTIC FORKS AND KN
SAWS, CAP'N CRUNCH, CHINESE FOOD TAKEOUT B
CAP, TOBLERONE, WALKMANS AND CASSETTE TA
FAKE LEGS, VIBRASLAPS, BRIDAL VEILS, STRINGS
TUXEDOS, SMALL CHIHUAHUAS, BANANA COSTUM

PLAYER), SIX-SHOOTER, FLOWERS, CANDLES, BLANK
EREALS, TWINKIES, MARSHMALLOWS, GUMBALLS +
EADPHONES AND MICROPHONE), FISHBOWLS, GIANT
AMERAS, ZYGOTE BALLS, BIRTHDAY CAKE, TAXICABS
T DOLLS, GLASSES OF WATER, ENVELOPES, TVS AND
RBLES, THIGHMASTERS, ROOMBAS, HEADDRESSES,
S AND KNIVES, CHRISTMAS TREES, POSTERS, SPACE
APHONES, FIRE EXTINGUISHERS, FIRE HOSES FILLED
BALLOONS FILLED WITH PAINT, HOOKAHS, STOOLS,
, WIZARD HATS, JESTER HAT, GRIM REAPER CLOAKS
CTOR BATONS, GLITTER, HEDGE TRIMMERS, LADY
RGENT, CYMBALS, LUMINESCENT AIRPLANE STICKS,
CISSORS, BOXES OF TISSUES, FLOWERS AND FLOWER
E INFLATABLE SHARKS, BOXING GLOVES, TORCHES
D WHIPS, LIGHTSABERS, SUPERMAN CAPES, WHITE
T ROLLERS, GINGERBREAD COOKIES, ICING, CANDY
TIC INNER TUBES, WORKING FIRE HYDRANTS, BEACH
LLS, THE CONEY ISLAND CYCLONE, MINI INFLATABLE
POGO STICKS, FOLEY SOUND EQUIPMENT, RUBBER
ASS SKIRTS, GOLF CLUBS CURLING SETS (FOR THE
ERS, SWIFFERS, DUCT TAPE, PLAY-DOH, HANDSAWS,
N WRAP, FEATHER DUSTERS, EGGNOG, IPHONES, SIRI
HONES, FAKE MUSTACHES, SUNGLASSES, SUNHATS
E PIÑATAS, FULL-SIZE PIÑATAS, FUN-SIZE SNICKERS
OOTBALL HELMETS, TREADMILLS, UMBRELLAS, CELL
LD, JASPER JOHNS'S *TARGET,* FUNNELS, STOP SIGNS,
IEFCASES, ROOM SERVICE CARTS, ELEVATOR FULL
AND, COCONUT DRINKS WITH UMBRELLAS, STUFFED
ECORATIONS, JIGSAWS, MULLET WIGS, VEGEMITE,
, PAINTING SUPPLIES OF ALL SORTS, BRAIN PROPS
PHONES, HARMONICAS, HARMONICA MICS (BULLET
CE MASKS, BIG GLOVES, SQUEEGEES, TYVEK SUITS,
, PLATES, LIGHTERS, HALOGEN LAMPS, ELECTRIC
, BANANAS, CHOPSTICKS, CLEAR PLASTIC SHOWER
CREAM CHEESE, LARGE BLACK FRAME GLASSES
OLIDAY LIGHTS, FOAM DUTCH SHOES, MONK ROBES
L STATIONS, TARPS, PINEAPPLES, IPHONE BOXES

COLLABORATORS: LUMINARIES

IN THE WESTERN WORLD and beyond, Blue Man Group has been observed with many well-known artists and cultural figures. Here is a small sampling of the notable figures recently documented with Blue Man Group.

FLOPPIE THE BANJO CLOWN

Perhaps one of the most distinguished luminaries to grant the Blue Men the pleasure of his collaborative talents is Floppie the Banjo Clown.

In interviews conducted between 1989 and 2003, rock-and-roll legends have had plenty to say about Floppie:

"I thought I knew how to rock, until I saw Floppie play. The show only lasted eleven seconds because he fell over and was injured and they carted him away. But that eleven seconds changed my life forever."
—RITCHIE BLACKMORE, GUITARIST, DEEP PURPLE

"I'm not even trying to rock anymore. It's been done to perfection. By Floppie."—CHRIS MARTIN, COLDPLAY

"He may be one of the first ever to do a vogue death drop. Except a good vogue dip is done on purpose, in time to the music. Ha! Sha-wham!" —RUPAUL, DRAG QUEEN

But just who was this clown? How did he come to influence thousands of famous rock acts all over the world? And how, despite his status as a rock legend, has he remained such a mystery after all of these years?
The late rock aficionado Justin Hardesty traveled the globe seeking answers to these questions. What he found through countless interviews, personal accounts, archive searches, and police records paints a vivid portrait of this odd, sad clown and how he became, and remains to this day, muse to many of our favorite rock-and-roll stars, including, apparently, Blue Man Group. For more on Floppie the Banjo Clown, see page 104.

A true Blue Man is joined by honorary Blue Man imposters Alan Ritchson and Joe Jonas.

In his youth Floppie's future seemed preordained to everyone but Floppie himself. He needed only to follow the obvious path before him: His look and pedigree made him a shoo-in for the party clown circuit. But alas it wasn't meant to be. The gods of rock and roll had spoken and Floppie heard the call. He had to go. Floppie's parents were devastated. Penniless and armed with only a cheap banjo and a fierce will to rock, Floppie hit the road to follow his rock-and-roll dreams. He was immediately arrested for vagrancy and thrown in jail.

Floppie made the best of prison life, entertaining the inmates with his unique hard rocking banjo style. With so much time on his hands Floppie honed his craft to perfection. He gave concerts and lessons. He started bands. He became a jailhouse hero. Floppie inspired the prisoners to be better people and to follow their dreams. And many of them did. Songs like "Give Up Your Shanks" and "It's Not Your Fault (Daddy Didn't Love You)" are credited with lowering prison assault rates due to their message and popularity.

Prison is prison however, and others soon started to use Floppie's influence for ill. In one famous incident the National Guard was brought in to break up the 1971 "flop-in riots." Hundreds of prisoners were falling flat on their backs imitating Floppie's now infamous backward flops to protest the prison conditions. The governor was forced to give in to the prisoner's demands.

"For six weeks the dang inmates would fall flat on their backs all day long! They started doing it during chow time on the tables and in the showers! One even self-immolated then flopped off the second story of the cellblock! It made one hell of a damn mess. I say good riddance to Flopsie the what's-his-face!"—Warden Donnie "Boo" Jeffries, Joliet State Correctional Facility

Upon his release the inmates, in a moment of silence, saluted Floppie with the now classic rock hand gesture as he walked out of jail a free clown. Many of the prisoners even started styling their hair in the "Floppie spikes" look we all know today in solidarity with their new hero and muse.

A ROCK LEGEND'S RISE... Back on the street, word spread in the vagabond world that a new messiah was among them. On street corners, under bridges, around burning tires, in alleyways and down by the tracks, Floppie would play for the downtrodden, the forgotten, the unwanted. He was a ray of light in an otherwise dark and perilous world.

One night in the back alley of a bar Floppie was discovered by a local rock band. They asked him to sit in on a couple of songs and power and energy in their sound. The only problem was that Floppie trashed their set. He kept falling flat on his back. He fell into

THE METEORIC RISE
AND TRAGIC FALL
OF A ROCK-AND-ROLL BANJO CLOWN

own good. The energy would over careening to the fl

Despite his malad Floppie to get notic gigs with local ban acts all wanted a pie came up with creativ pie on his feet. On a t with Rammstein they to a giant, fire-breathi rolled him around the st

...AND FINAL FLOP Trag Banjo Clown's meteoric r climbed onto a stack of M started to rock unimagin rest is history. "We were d About To Rock,' it was on favorites. No one saw him amps. When we finally notic late. I blame myself really. than a friend to me. He was m on rocking, Floppie. I shall m Angus Young, guitarist, AC/DC

WHAT DOES THIS UBIQUITOUS ROCK CONCERT HAND GESTURE MEAN?

Speculation abounds as to its origins and meaning.

Although some say it originated in ancient times as a gesture used to ward off evil spirits, it is recognized most in modern culture as the symbol for rock. The gesture was popularized by Black Sabbath front man Ronnie James Dio when he replaced outgoing lead singer Ozzy Osbourne. Dio won't take credit for inventing the gesture however, only its proliferation.

But a growing contingent believes that when rock concert fans make this hand gesture they are actually paying homage to the late, legendary rock figure Floppie the Banjo Clown.

MAKING THE FLOPPIE THE BANJO CLOWN HAND PUPPET

According to rock legend Jason Mackenroth, the hand puppet gesture is easily made.[2] Simply raise your arm, palm facing forward. Fold middle fingers down leaving your pinky and index fingers raised. Grip the folded fingers with your thumb. For a slight variation, extend thumb outward (Gene Simmons of Kiss used the thumb-out version to great effect).

Here are some popular variations:

THE BASIC FLOPPIE FLASH

45°

20°

FLOPPIE FLASH WITH HEAD BANG
Helps to have shit loads of hair.

DOUBLE FLOPPIE

DOUBLE FLOPPIE WITH TONGUE HANG
(See: Gene Simmons)
Can also be executed with a Basic Floppie Flash

FLOPPIE CROSS
Often seen with Tongue Hang.

INVERTED FLOPPIE CROSS

130°

THE CUT-TIME FLOPPIE
Slightly more advanced. Good for mosh pits.

THE REVERSED TWO-HAND FLOPPIE
Also known as the "Mega Floppie"; for when a single-hand Basic Floppie won't quite cut it.

the amps, the drum kit, the keyboard; he broke half of our gear. He was a total spaz. We got booed pretty hard but for about eleven seconds there we never sounded better!"
—Dale Powers, associate kitchen supervisor, Red Lobster, Inc.

Floppie's Kryptonite was his inability to re-main physically upright during his performanc-es. He simply became too excited while he played and would fall over, usually flat on his back. Some say it was his oversized shoes that made it difficult to stand others contend his enormous head of hair made him top heavy. One crazy theory has it that genetically, clowns in general have very little balance to speak of. But most will tell you that Floppie simply rocked too hard for his body, his power of his rock band, sending him

It didn't take long for word of Floppie's talented booking in the bigger Stagehands keep Flop-pie from Europe kidnapped him wagon and he played.

Floppie the short. dalia he years and The those Floppie's the too were p

① Floppie was buried next to Jim Morrison of the Doors in an unmarked grave at Père Lachaise Cemetery in Paris, France. His remains were later moved to Schnectady, NJ by a devout group of Floppie fanatics, where he was buried beneath a magnificent headstone, pictured opposite.
② Blue Man Group cannot be held responsible for any injury including but not limited to repet-itive motion injury sustained during attempted Floppie the Banjo Clown hand puppet moves and the Floppie the Banjo Clown hand puppet practitioner assumes all responsibility herein, in perpetuity throughout the universe.

COLLABORATORS: RITUAL PARTICIPANTS

PERHAPS THE SINGLE MOST IMPORTANT GROUP of Blue Man collaborators are know any meaning or purpose without this vital crowd of people.

These participants seem to gather in the Blue Man space in hopes of creating euphori

It is a delicate balance of two strange worlds coming together in one sublime locatio intricate, symbiotic relationship between the two. It is this exciting emotional and chemi makes the ritualistic happening come to life.

...s the "ritual participants." It is fair to question whether the ritual would have

...nnections via the shared experience within.

The success of the union relies on an

reaction that

TUBES PERMEATE THE BLUE MAN WORLD and have often been known to infiltrate the ritual itself. The proliferation of tubes might simply convey a love of plumbing.

To the untrained eye, the proliferation of tubes might simply convey a love of plumbing.

Plumbing pipes, electrical conduits, transportation systems, and computer networks allow us to see in physical form the many systems that bind members of an urban society together.

STUFF:
TUBES

It has been speculated that conduits of all types may serve as a metaphor for the paradox of modern urban design— we are more connected yet more separate than ever before.

However, without concrete proof, the true significance of tubes must continue to be regarded as open for interpretation.

Some see the circulatory system and neural pathways as similar representations of connective systems.

TUBE TALKERS

Early participants in the Blue Man rituals describe a system of tubes that connected their seats with a mysterious space beyond. A voice from within the tube engaged them in conversation, connecting strangers to faceless strangers.

STUFF:
FRACTALS

OVER THE YEARS, the Blue Men have shown a particular interest in fractal© images.

Some believe their interest is based on the observation that fractals evoke both science and art in equal parts.

Others speculate that the Blue Men are drawn to these voluptuous biomorphic shapes because they seem to resonate with the primordial exuberance of life itself.

①A fractal is a natural phenomenon (or a mathematical set) that exhibits a repeating pattern. This pattern displays at every scale. ①A fractal is a natural phenomenon (or a mathematical set) that exhibits a repeating pattern. This pattern displays at every scale. ①A fractal is a natural phenomenon (or a mathematical set) that exhibits a repeating pattern. This pattern displays at every scale. ①A fractal is a natural phenomenon (or a mathematical set) that exhibits a repeating pattern. This pattern displays at every scale.

STUFF:
ANIMATION

ZOETROPE

From the Greek *zoe* for "life" and *tropos,* "turning." Developed in the nineteenth century, the zoetrope is an animation device that appears to bring inanimate objects to life.

Blue Men use a 3-D stroboscopic sculptural zoetrope conceived by Herbert Hoover[1] to "bring to life" twelve drumming figures.[2]

"THE WORD "ANIMATION" comes from the Latin word *animare,* which toward bringing art to life has been around since the dawn of civilization. Animation as we now know it began in Europe in the 1830s with of a simple principle—when a picture is flashed in front of your eyes, you retained in your mind will meld together creating the illusion of movement. The Blue Men seem to enjoy exploring the idea

The Blue Men have also been known to illustrate animation via the intricacies of Indonesian shadow puppetry.[3]

CAVE PAINTINGS OF LASCAUX

These 20,000-year-old cave paintings depict a wild boar in two different positions superimposed over each other. Scientists believe that the flickering fire-light used in the cave may have created a simple animation effect.

means "to bring to life." It could be argued that the artistic impulse It is perhaps no surprise that the Blue Men share this impulse.

the invention of the zoetrope. The zoetrope took advantage retain a temporary after-image. In any kind of animation, the after images This physiological phenomenon is called persistence of vision.

of "bringing to life" via this quirk of physiology.

①Not the president. ②Although somewhat reminiscent of the lonely, isolated Giacometti figures, these sculptural beings are instead united in a circle and exhibit signs of joyful ritualistic connection. ③Invented in the first century AD, Indonesian shadow puppetry is also considered a precursor to modern-day animation. These stylized characters were brought to life by incredibly skilled puppeteers who spent decades mastering the subtlety and nuance of this delicate art form.

signs into their spaces and rituals. The significance of these signs has been the mysterious and enchanting.

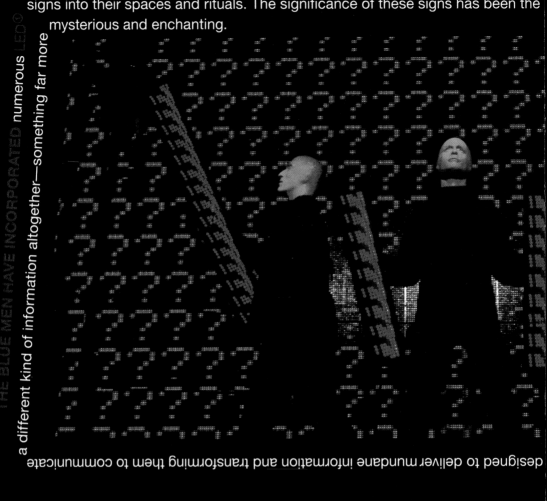

THE BLUE MEN HAVE INCORPORATED numerous LED⊕ a different kind of information altogether—something far more

designed to deliver mundane information and transforming them to communicate

topic of ongoing speculation. The most

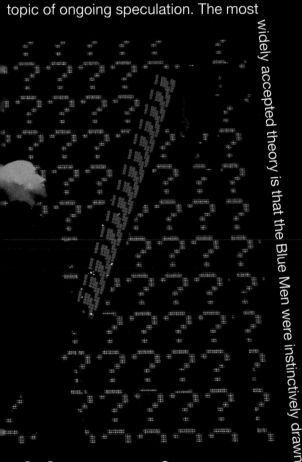

widely accepted theory is that the Blue Men were instinctively drawn to the idea of taking utilitarian moving signs

Art historian Mimi Yu writes, "I can't help but feel Blue Man Group's use of modern information systems is evocative of the work of Jenny Holzer. Her installations speak the language of mass communication while broadcasting disturbing, thought-provoking content that asks us to consider what we discuss, what we repress, and what messages we accept from the powers that be."[2]

Volcanologist Timothy Quinn adds, "Personally, I'm reminded of hot, vibrant magma streams. I get caught up in the trancelike energy of flowing lava, like watching molten iron poured in a forge. The slow, steady motion, the realization that if we watch long enough, we just might witness nature's extraordinary, mysterious process of transformation."

Average gal Ellie Cunningham observes, "Is it possible we're overthinking this? Aren't LEDs just cool?"

[1] LED: light emitting diode. [2] Jenny Holzer is an American artist known for her large-scale installation projects exploring the use of words and ideas in public spaces.

STUFF:
COLLOIDS/
TRANSMOGRIFICATION

GAS

SOLID

LIQUID

SHAVING CREAM
is a gas dispersed within a liquid (liquid foam)

PAINT
is a solid suspended in a liquid (sol); is also a hydrocolloid

FOG
is a liquid dispersed within a gas

JELL-O
is a liquid dispersed in a solid (gel)

THE BLUE MEN APPEAR TO HAVE A PARTICULAR FASCINATION

with various types of colloidal suspensions, or as they are sometimes referred to in the vernacular, "gooey substances."①

MARSHMALLOW
is air suspended in a
solid (solid foam)

AIR

TWINKIES

Even Twinkies are a colloid. Those in the colloid community view Twinkies to be among the most advanced colloid known to man, in that it is everything suspended in everything.

①See also The Moment of Bifurcation, page 154.

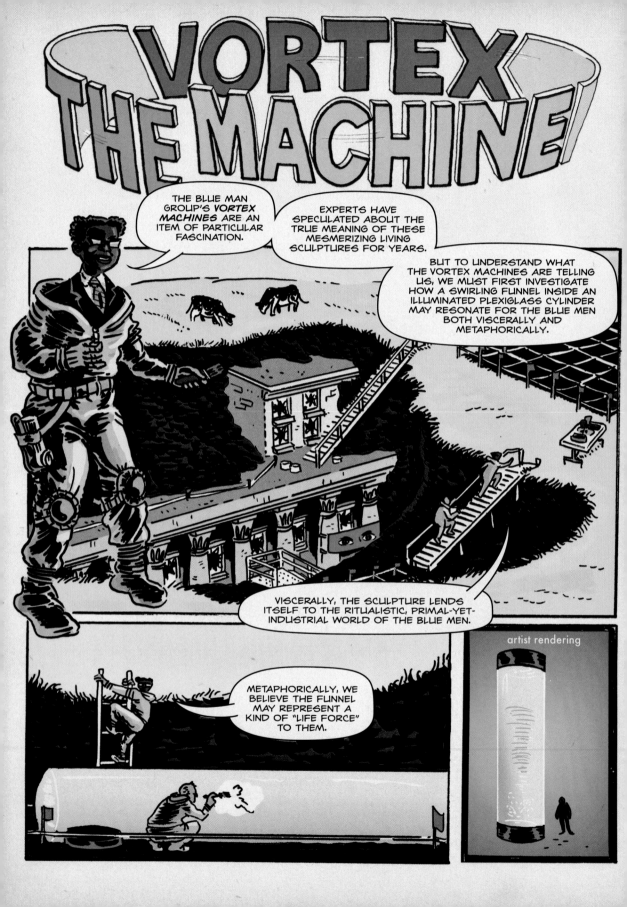

ARMED WITH PRIGOGINE'S ODEL, ONE CAN SEE THAT THE ORTEX IS MUCH MORE THAN A METAPHOR.
IT IS A TALE OF MYTHIC PROPORTIONS-- A STORY THAT TELLS US THAT THE PROCESS OF TRANSFORMATION IS NOT WITHOUT RISK.
THE MESSAGE OF THE VORTEX MACHINE IS QUITE CLEAR -- NO BENEFIT CAN COME FROM TURNING BACK THE MOMENT THINGS START TO FEEL OFF BALANCE.
UNLESS WE ARE WILLING TO PUSH THROUGH THAT HARROWING POINT, WE WILL NEVER REACH A HIGHER LEVEL OF STABILITY.
IN LIFE, JUST AS IN THE BLUE MAN RITUALS--IT MAY NOT ALWAYS BE CLEAR IF OUR EFFORTS ARE MOVING US CLOSER TO STABILITY.
BUT IF WE CAN TRUST ENOUGH TO TURN THE MOTOR ON HIGH AND LEAVE IT ON, TURN UP THE VOLUME, AND HOLD ON TIGHT--
THE FUNNEL WILL SHOW UP.

STUFF:
VORTEX
MACHINES

126

**WHEN
THE
VORTEX
HAS
FULLY
FORMED**
it is
typically
a sign
that the
ritual is
about
to
begin.

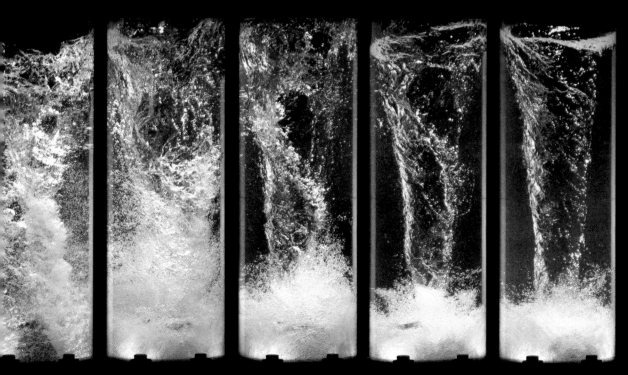

SECTION 3
BLUE MAN
RITUALS

IT IS TIME FOR AN INQUIRY INTO THE CURIOUS, ENIGMATIC RITUALS OF BLUE MAN GROUP.

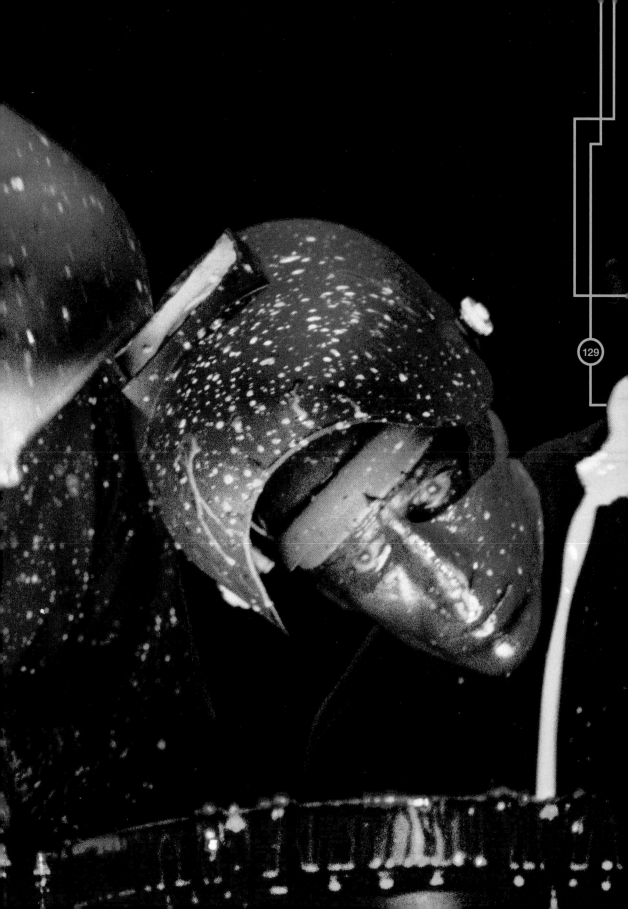

EVOCATION

HOW—and why—does a Blue Man ritual begin?

Some believe that the Blue Men set their own ritual into motion, inviting strangers to join them. Others subscribe to a theory that it is the collective unconscious[1] that creates the necessary conditions for a ritual to commence. When the Blue Men sense the need for the ritual, they arrive to facilitate.

What "need" might this be?

New Abstraction Gallery Curator Ruth Elaine speculates that the Blue Men share an affinity with the abstract expressionists in this regard. According to Robert Motherwell[2]: "nothing as drastic an innovation as abstract art could have come into existence without a most profound, relentless, unquenchable need. The need is for felt experience—intense, immediate, direct, subtle, unified, warm, vivid, and rhythmic… Abstract art is a true mysticism, or rather a series of mysticisms that grew up in the historical circumstance that all mysticisms do, from a primary sense of a gulf, an abyss, a void, between one's lonely self and the world. Abstract art is an effort to close the void that modern humans feel."

Many kinds of artists have reflected on the theme of modern urban isolation.

Some inventors have seemingly embraced the idea and taken it to the next level. Here, Hugo Gernsback explores an extreme form of urban isolation, with his invention of The Isolator. The contraption attempts to not only focus an employee's mind when working, but also to shield them from the time-consuming nuisance of having to engage in conversation or create meaningful connections with coworkers.

③

① Also known as "the collective pretentious." For more on Carl Jung, see page 137. ② Robert Motherwell (1915–1991) was an American abstract expressionist artist. Other abstract expressionists include: Jackson Pollock, Mark Rothko, and Willem de Kooning. All were known for their bold, exuberant paintings and for their drunken salons* at the Cedar Tavern. *A salon is a gathering of persons noted in literature, philosophy, the fine arts or similar areas, to discuss important topics and drink. Cedar Tavern was a popular New York City hang out for beatnik writers and abstract expressionist artists. The establishment eventually banned Jackson Pollock for tearing a bathroom door off its hinges and hurling it at fellow artist Franz Kline during one of their frequent disagreements. The Cedar Tavern closed its doors in 2006.

ANATOMY
OF A RITUAL

EVERY ONE OF BLUE MAN GROUP'S ritualistic happenings is unique, however, they do follow a similar composition and set of patterns shared by rituals of other groups throughout history.

Erdal Atintop, anthropologist and expert in the field of Blue Man studies, has divided the Blue Man ritual into three distinct phases:

PHASE 1: THE REVEAL
Here we meet the Blue Men for the first time.

PHASE 2: CULTURAL EXCHANGE
We encounter the Blue Men and begin to learn about their ways as they begin to learn about ours. Our worlds begin to mesh.

PHASE 3: THE UNIFIED GROUP EUPHORIA
Participants feel themselves a part of a new community, a wholeness that feels greater than the sum of its parts.

Throughout history many popular rituals have included gathering around a fire and communing with others.

Ancient campfire ritual

Tailgating ritual

LIFE FORCE

Scientists studying Blue Man Group acknowledge that their rituals have an extraordinary effect on the Blue Men and the humans who are present. Some claim to sense a shift in individual energy as well as a change in the overall space. Can this effect be quantified?

In his seminal work *Blue in the Face*[1], Atintop wrote: "In order to pinpoint the effect of the Blue Man ritual, I created several scientific instruments to measure what I call 'life force.'[2] Life force is that which gives something its vitality or strength; the spirit or energy that animates things. Through my studies I've been able to identify key moments where the life force simmers, spikes, builds, accelerates, or erupts at various points in a Blue Man ritual."

While Atintop's work regarding the life force is fairly recent, artists have attempted to illustrate this intangible exuberance throughout history.[3] For example, Some believe that the Bauhaus dance image, seen here, is the early life force exploration of Dr. Atintop.[4]

[1] A collection of essays later made into a motion picture starring Kevin Klein, Harrison Ford, and John Cleese as the Blue Men, subsequently remade with Kristen Wiig, Amy Poehler, and Emma Stone in the same roles. [2] Atintop has acknowledged that the idea of Life Force is inspired by the concept of qi, from traditional Chinese medicine and martial arts. The same force is known as prana in the Hindu religion, ki in Japanese culture, gi in Korea culture, mana in traditional Hawaiian culture, and the Force in Comic-Con culture. Other activities that cause noticeable spikes in life force include action painting, most sports but especially competitive Ping-Pong and synchronized swimming, human reproduction, bungee jumping, karaoke, swimming in freezing cold water, competitive dancing, REM dreaming, 3 log rolling, and hunting Easter eggs. [3] Life force was also famously explored in the work of Yves Klein. See page 157. [4] Others argue that this image is just further proof that no costume party can ever compare to the ones thrown by Oskar Schlemmer and his Bauhaus friends.

PHASE 1:
IN SHADOWS

THE FIRST TIME MOST PARTICIPANTS IN THE RITUAL SEE THE BLUE MEN, THEY APPEAR IN SHADOW.

Theater anthropologist Thomas K. Scott III, speculates, "I believe the Blue Men use shadows to create a mood of timeless mystery. The shadows also serve to ease the transition, helping the viewers gradually acclimate into the intense energy of the Blue Men."

Blue Man Insider Wyatt Falardeau believes the metaphor is clear, "The Blue Men are obviously taking the audience on a Jungian① journey into the collective unconscious by using the 'shadow' as a metaphor for the primal self that gets repressed by the modern persona."

Average guy Robbie Vail is quick to disagree, "I don't even understand what that means."

①Referring to C. G. Jung, Swiss psychiatrist and psychotherapist known as the father of analytical psychology, founded on the idea of individuation, which refers to the development of the individual as being distinct from the general, collective group. Jung also coined the phrases and ideas behind some of the most well known concepts of psychology, including the collective unconscious, extroversion and introversion, and the complex.*

*In this case, "the complex" refers to the belief that the most important factors influencing one's personality are deep in the unconscious. This is not to be confused with the name of an album of recorded Blue Man Group music of the same name.

BLUE
MAN
GROUP

THE COMPLEX

PHASE 1:
UN
MASKED
MEN

IN REGARD TO the persona, *The Conduit* handbook reflects: "As human beings, we are born with an innate curiosity and sense of wonder about the world around us. As we grow and mature, this natural inclination to explore begins to ebb as the processes of socialization work on our psyches. A persona[1] develops out of the need to protect ourselves from this vulnerability. For many, the persona masks the true self and the innocent, vulnerable, childlike curiosity from birth is covered up entirely, cutting us off from those around us. But persona is a mask, not a replacement for one's true self."

Noted theater anthropologist and Blue Man Insider Joe Burke, professor emeritus of culture at Wink University, speculates: "Some people believe the Blue Men are humans wearing a mask. But in my mind, it is the opposite. The Blue Men represent what humans might be like without a cultural mask. Their rituals offer us a glimpse of what it might feel like to live without our cultural persona—a life free of the mask."[2]

EVERY MORNING, I PUT IT ON
I WALK OUTSIDE, AND I AM GONE
AND I DON'T SEEM TO MIND ANYMORE
I CAN'T THINK WHAT IT WAS LIKE BEFORE
I WORE IT ALL THE TIME

IN THE EVENING, I TAKE IT OFF
BUT THERE'S ANOTHER ONE UNDERNEATH
AND I CAN'T SEEM TO FIND THE BOTTOM OF THE STACK
I MIGHT JUST LOSE MY MIND AND NEVER GET IT BACK
BUT AT LEAST I'LL GET INSIDE

THERE'S A FEELING THAT I GET SOMETIMES
IT'S SO SMALL THAT IT'S EASY TO HIDE
IT'S LIKE A HOWLING VOICE FROM A DISTANT PAST
IT SEEMS I'VE GOT NO CHOICE WHEN IT COMES TO THIS
IT'S BUILDING UP INSIDE ③

① Persona refers to the image or personality one exhibits and that shapes others' perception of the self.* ② In regard to the "true self," Burke often references a quote from art critic and art historian Donald Kuspit: "I think of a work of art as a toy for adults…The adult uses the toy…to make the transition back to the interior reality he or she tends to forget in his or her dealings with exterior reality. It evokes a self that has been hidden so successfully that the adult tends to forget he or she has it. That regression—I tend to think of it as the recovery of a buried treasure—is no doubt risky and dangerous, but it is ultimately refreshing and revitalizing."† *Many artists have created alternative characters in an effort to free themselves of any creative constraints, or preconceived ideas about their more famous persona. For example, David Bowie's Ziggy Stardust, Garth Brooks's Chris Gaines, and Beyoncé's Sasha Fierce. †Kuspit, Donald (2001, June). The Romantic Subject. Artnet ③ Lyrics associated with a particular Blue Man Group song, aptly titled "Persona"

PHASE 1:
MUTUAL OBSERVATION PERIOD

AS RITUAL PARTICIPANTS OBSERVE THE BLUE MEN, they realize that the Blue Men are also observing them, searching the space for clues about the wider culture.

Studies show that if you make four minutes of un-
interrupted eye contact with somebody, you might
fall in love with them.[1]

[1] Dr. Arthur Aron of Stony Brook University developed a study of
how sustained eye contact leads to feelings of love using a question-
naire and method to determine feelings of closeness and intimacy
between two strangers.

PHASE 1:
INFORMATION OVERLOAD

WHEN THE BLUE MEN
look into our world, what
might they see?

143

PHASE 1:
A CAUTIOUS
INVITATION

GRADUALLY, IT BEGINS TO FEEL as though the Blue Men are reaching out to us, if cautiously.

"If you would like to establish a connection with people from another culture, it's always good to offer a few gifts as a gesture of friendship. But, an even better way

"to forge a lasting bond is by creating something together. Whether it's a meal, an art project, or just a spontaneous dance party, when you create with others, you build a connection that lasts a lifetime". —from *The Social Synapse* by Nora Epinephrine and Sarah Tonin

PHASE 2: BLESH

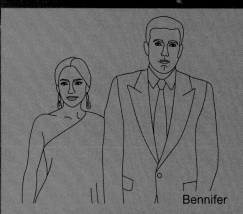

Bennifer

A portmanteau is a linguistic "bleshing" in which parts of words, or their sounds, are put together to form a new word that encapsulates key parts of both separate words. It is colloquially referred to as a "frankenword," a stitching together of seemingly unrelated words to create something never seen before.⑥

THE SECOND PHASE of a Blue Man experience is the joining of the Blue Man world with the human world, which Dr. Atintop calls "bleshing."[1]

The word "blesh"[2] is a portmanteau[3] that combines the words "blend" and "mesh"[4] to describe how individuals can at times combine their talents and attention in such a way that they appear to behave as a single organism.[5]

[1] All due respect to Dr. Atintop, now that we've defined the concept, can we all agree not to use this word again? [2] First used in Theodore Sturgeon's 1953 novel *More Than Human,* which followed six people with extraordinary powers who were able to "blesh" their abilities and in this way operate as one single organism. In the story, they progress toward a mature gestalt consciousness, referred to in this fantasy world as the "homo gestalt," the next step in human evolution. [3] See sidebar. [4] Some people think the word is a melding of "blush" and "flesh," which would just be weird. [5] See siphonophores, page 33. [6] "Portmanteau" was introduced in this vocabular sense by Lewis Carroll in *Through the Looking-Glass.* Humpty Dumpty explains to Alice that a portmanteau is two meanings packed into one word. Lithe + Slimy = Slithy. Fuming + Furious = Flumious. Modern examples include: Hungry + Angry = Hangry and Shih Tzu + Poodle = Shitzapoo.

PHASE 2:
TECHNOLOGY

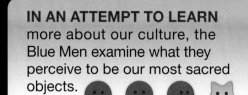

IN AN ATTEMPT TO LEARN more about our culture, the Blue Men examine what they perceive to be our most sacred objects.

Even the Blue Man cannot resist a great selfie.

ice

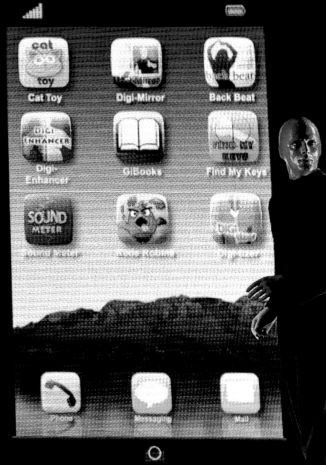

Cat Toy

Digi-Mirror

Back Beat

Digi-Enhancer

GiBooks

Find My Keys

Sound Meter

Phone

Messaging

Mail

PHASE 2: SHARING A MEAL

THE BLUE MEN have been known to try their hand at one of humanity's most common social rituals: sharing a meal. Their attempts to capture the nuances of our cultural mores are sometimes undermined by their incomplete understanding of our ways as well as their unique physiology. But, their intention is clear: to forge a deeper connection.

Viewed through the lens of a Blue Man ritual, the making of a satisfying dining experience includes:

COLLOIDS

A FREEDOM FROM PESKY INSECTS

ART

THE PROPER ENVIRONMENT

PHASE 2: BURSTING WITH JOY

FOR FURTHER REFERENCE
see, The Moment of Bifurcation,
page 154.

PHASE 2:
THE MOMENT
OF BIFURCATION

A FEW BLUE MAN OBSERVERS have noted an intriguing, temporary sensation of discomfort; a moment where their personal boundaries and beliefs about social decorum may be challenged. This moment, which differs for everyone, is often followed by a new perspective and feeling of connection.

Those who have studied the Blue Men at great length refer to this moment as the "bifurcation point," the point at which a system will either fly out of control or transform itself in a new level of stability.[1]

Blue Man expert Manny L. Friedman observes, "What is fascinating to me is that the Blue Men remain completely innocent[2] and unaware of the preconceived ideas we may have. The Blue Men don't seem to have any judgment or concern about what they are exploring. I imagine it is much like embarking on a scientific exploration for them, and we willingly follow. Although at times surprising, these moments challenge us to wiggle and giggle and squirm through our glorious discomfort, and trust that we'll all leap together into a new energetic order."

Even eye contact has a bifurcation point. Eye contact held longer than seven seconds can begin to create discomfort. But it is often just beyond that moment, if you stay with it, that something wonderful can happen.[3]

①For more on the Vortex Machine, see page 198. ②See Dr. Irving Bock's Modality Theory and his explanation of "Innocent," page 48. ③For more regarding falling love through prolonged eye contact, see page 81.

PHASE 2:
COLLABORATION

FURTHER EVIDENCE OF OUR CULTURAL EXCHANGE may be observed when the Blue Men invite a guest to join them in the act of creation and collaboration. The Blue Men appear to play the role of painter and their guest plays the role of paintbrush.

The bond between the ritual participant and the Blue Men seems to be forever sealed by this cocreation of art.

SERGEI
PRETENCIONE

Although his work came much later, Italian performance artist Sergei Pretencione claims it was actually *he* who first created a "life force" painting. As of this printing Sergei Pretencione is in the midst of a brand-new piece entitled *Run*, which involves the artist avoiding arrest after stealing priceless furniture from the Vatican.

①Called anthropometry—the use of people as "human paintbrushes." In this case, the Blue Men use a technique often credited to French artist Yves Klein, who spent his life attempting to capture a visceral experience of life force. He first tried to capture this force in action paintings. Later, he tried to convey it through monochromatic paintings—most famously, all-blue canvases.* Finally, Klein created an installation of pure, empty space—a void.† ***Yves Klein invented his own ultra-intense color blue. He loved blue for its connection to the sky, the sea, and the heavens, the idea of the infinite. He once said "blue is the invisible becoming visible."** In 1958, three thousand people lined up to see an exhibition mounted by Klein of an empty room called Le Vide (The Void), where he claimed his paintings were now invisible. "The Void" eventually became a term used to describe a Zen-like state devoid of material possessions and worldly influences. In 1960, Klein staged a photograph entitled *Leap into the Void*, that featured Klein leaping headfirst into space. An unsubstantiated photograph seems to capture the Blue Men assisting Klein's leap. (See page 13.) Although some claim this photograph was faked using Photoshop, the photo was clearly taken before Photoshop existed. Whether or not the photograph is real, the Blue Men do often leap into an unknown, potentially volatile, environment: the crowd of strangers is experiencing their ritual. **†In this case, "The Void" is not believed to be the same "void" of which Motherwell spoke on page 132, but, as with all artistic expressions, it is open to interpretation.**

REFLECTION

AT THIS JUNCTURE, just before the third phase of the ritual, the Blue Men often take a moment to pause. In this moment of reflection, they are surrounded by darkness.

They glow in the kind of light that can only be fully appreciated in true darkness.

Blue Man expert Betty Holt interprets the significance of this instant, "Whether it's stars, sparks, firelight, or fireflies, there is a certain kind of magic that these bioluminescent beings provide. Maybe it's a metaphor for something greater, some illumination from within, some life force, I don't know. I just know I am completely drawn in and utterly enchanted by this moment."

PHASE 3:
THE UNIFIED GROUP EUPHORIA

It is interesting to note that other uses of the word "gestalt" may also be applicable to the Blue Man Group ritual.

Gestalt therapy focuses on the individual's experience in the present moment and attempts to understand the formation of meaningful perceptions in an apparently fragmented world.

Gestalt cuisine is an emerging field of molecular gastronomy in which chefs attempt to combine ingredients in such a way that renders the original food unrecognizable. The results are both flabbergasting and delicious.

DR. ATINTOP LABELED the third and final phase of the Blue Man rituals "unified group euphoria."① In this phase, the energy rises, and the participants begin to spontaneously engage in collective behavior, as if a single organism. Psychiatrist Stewart Jackson observes, "It's as if the entire group has passed through a bifurcation point and leapt gleefully and unabashedly headfirst into a gestalt!"

① When asked how to explain the difference between "gestalt" and "party," Dr. Atintop responded, "First of all, gestalt is harder to pronounce, and second... Well come to think of it, they're not all that different (assuming it's a *really* good party)."

PHASE 3:
ECSTATIC TRANCE

IN THE FINAL PHASE of the ritual, the contagious energy of the Blue Men spreads to the participants causing them to break out into spontaneous yet synchronized movements expressing both elation and a desire to follow instructions.

Time to start.
These graphics describe the ritualistic movements groups often exhibit.

Movement # 1
The Basic
Head Bob

Movement # 2
The One Armed
Fist Pump

Movement # 3
The Up and Down
Jumping Motion

Movement # 4
The Behind the
Head Leg Stretch

Movement # 5
Wave Your Hands
in the Air Like You
Just Don't Care

Movement # 6
The Two Arm Upward
Thrust with Yell

Movement # 7
Raise the Roof

① Although no evidence can be found to substantiate this rumor, it is worth noting that hundreds of witnesses describe a Blue Man ritual wherein crowds of people began an impromptu sing-along of Jefferson Airplane's "White Rabbit"* as if on cue. *The potential significance of this song choice has been thoroughly investigated. No viable connection to the Blue Man ritual can be found.

PHASE 3:
THE BAND DANCES

THE APEMAN

IT IS NOT UNCOMMON to catch a glimpse o

THE ZOMBIE

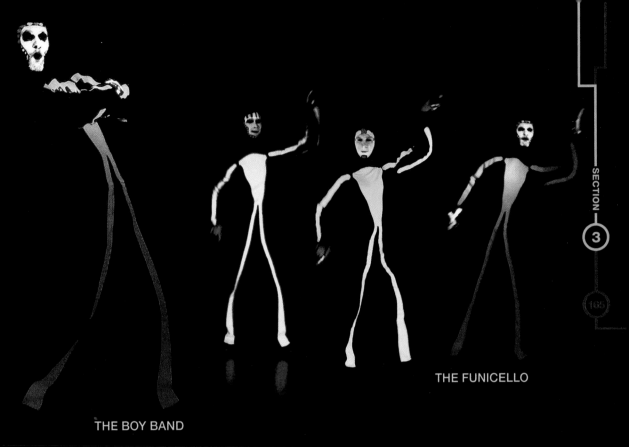

THE BOY BAND

THE FUNICELLO

...he Band performing their own celebratory body movements.

...E TRAVOLTA

THE THRILLER

LARGE GROUPS OF PEOPLE HAVE B

BODIES, MOST NOTABLY, THEIR POSTE

BACKSIDE, BOTTOM, BUTTOCKS, JUNK

TART, FANNY, DOUBLE SLUG, WIGGL

FLESH POT, SECOND FACE, BOUNCE

MEDICINE BALL, SONIC BOOM, SIT BI

COOKER, SUBWOOFER, HORN SECTIO

THE CLOSER, CROCK-POT, JUMBOTRO

WITH NO TUSKS, GEORGE FOREMAN

WHERE ALL THE BURRITOS GO, GIANT

PAUL, FLAB CABBAGE, BUN PUPPETS,

WIGGLE MONKEYS, GRIPPER, TWEED

DIABLO, CANADA, GELATINOUS AVAT

GROWING PERSONAL FOLLOWING, B

YOUR FLOUNDER THAT'S ROUNDER T

END, JELLY POT, J. LO'S, LIFE'S WORK

TWO BULBOUS FRIENDS, CABOOSE, I

COUSINS, SEAT SOCKET, GROSS DOM

MUFFIN, SMILING BULLDOG, RUMP-H

IN THE DANCE PARTY ARSENAL, CAP

HEINIE, KEISTER, TUSH, BUNS, BUM

CLUSTER, FRODO, JOHN MADDEN,

BONELESS FRIENDS, ALI VS. FRAZIE

MONSTER TRUCK, SKIN SMURF, WIG

...N WITNESSED MOVING THEIR ENTIRE
...OR, ALSO KNOWN AS: **HINDQUARTERS,**
THE TRUNK, BADONKADONK, SQUASH
BAGS, MUD FLAPS, RUMP ROCKETS,
...OUSE, JIGGLE TWINS, BUBBLE POP,
...UIT, MUMBLER, ROCK TUMBLER, FUN
...LAUNCHPAD, MOTHRA, THE OUTBACK,
WAFFLE IRON, BOOTY, HAPPY WALRUS
...ILL, MY DINNER WITH ANDRE, PLACE
...UFFY BEARS, MINNEAPOLIS AND SAINT
GANTOR, TWO MOUNDS OF MISCHIEF,
...DEE AND TWEEDLEDUM, HIPSTER, EL
..., FLUBBER CHUNKS, PANTS PILLOW,
...OMWHACKER, REPORTER AT LARGE,
...N A GIANT QUARTER POUNDER, REAR
...DANCE CAPTAIN, CARRY-ON LUGGAGE,
...NK FURNACE, THE BLOB, TWO WEIRD
...TIC PRODUCT, THAT THANG, FRECKLE
...MP, JUMP-PUMP, GREATEST WEAPON
...IN JIGGLENAUTS, RUMP, POSTERIOR,
...CAKES, JAR JAR BINKS, CHOCOLATE
...MOSCOW, ROTUNDA, AIRBAGS, TWO
ELVIS AARON PRESLEY, BUTTERCUP
...E CLOWN, BUTT, YOUR TRUMP RUMP

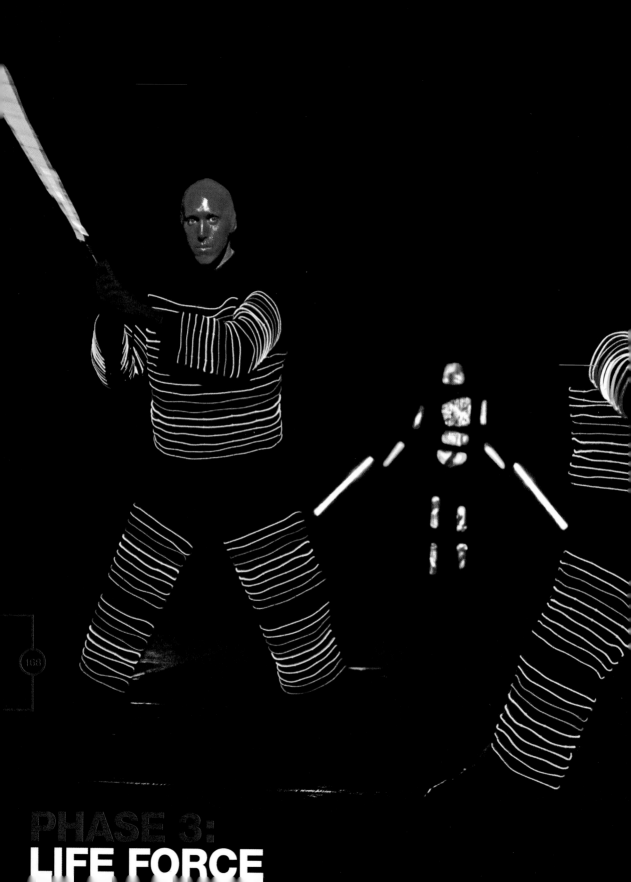

PHASE 3:
LIFE FORCE

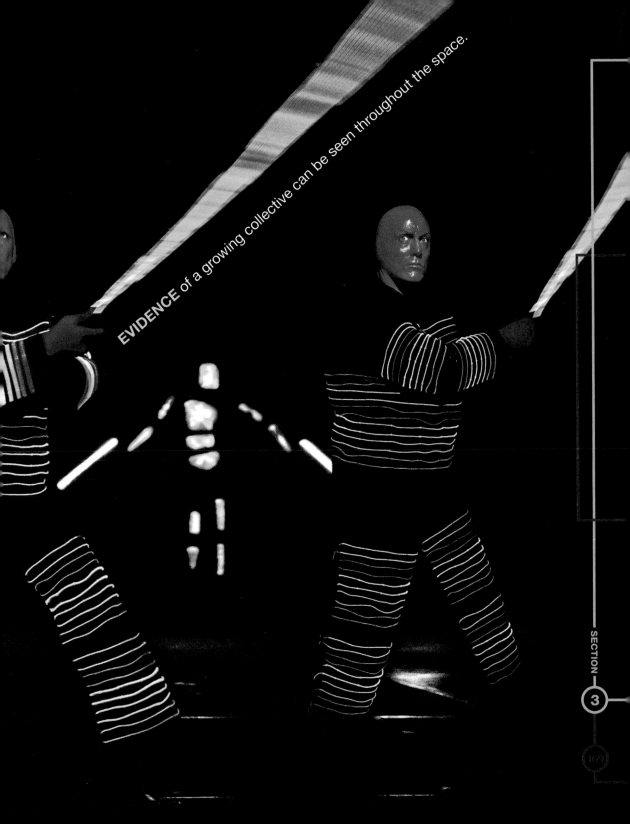

EVIDENCE of a growing collective can be seen throughout the space.

PHASE 3:
LIFE FORCE

172

PHASE 3:
LIFE FORCE

PHASE 3:
COLLECTIVE SYNESTHESIA

SOME WITNESSES CLAIM to suddenly experience the visual ability of the Blue Men, including the ability to "see" what a drumbeat looks like . . .

COLLECTIVE
SYNESTHESIA

...OR THE ABILITY TO SEE EMOTIONS. The more elation is present, the more illumination we see...

PHASE 3:
COLLECTIVE SYNESTHESIA

COLLECTIVE
SYNESTHESIA

180

CONNECTIVITY

...STILL OTHERS CLAIM to have a temporary visual understanding of how we as people and, in fact, all things on earth are connected.

PHASE 3:
CONNECTIVITY

186

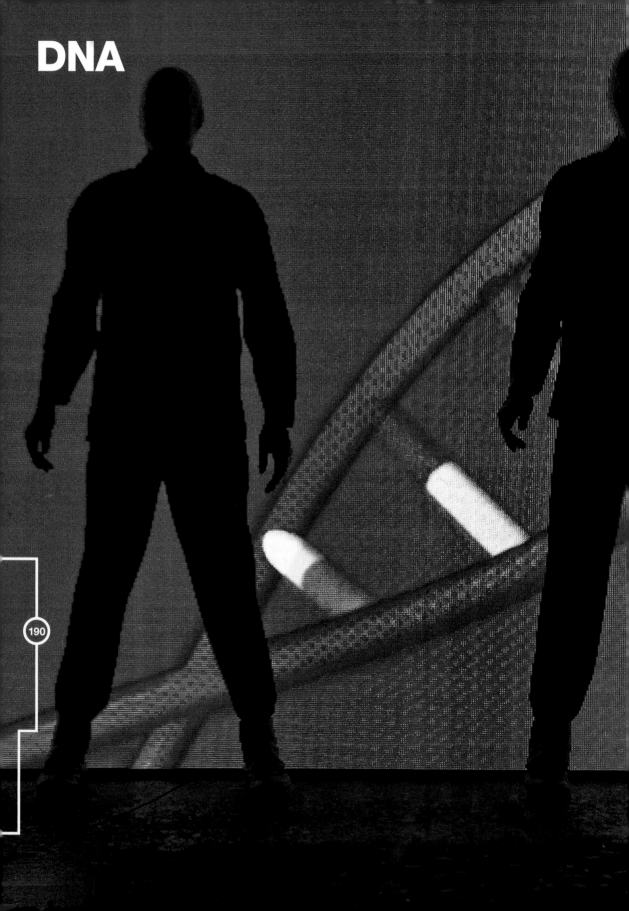

DNA

often end their ritual
waving from within a spiraling
strand of human DNA.
This has led some to speculate
that the Blue Men
are not so different from us,
not so "other" after all . . .

PERHAPS
they are instead
the part of
each of us
that wants to
play, explore,
connect,
and celebrate life
in all its gooey
and mysterious
splendor.

splendor.
and mysterious
in all its gooey
and celebrate life
connect,
play, explore,
that wants to
each of us
the part of
they are instead
PERHAPS

GLOSSARY

anarchist: 1. One who believes in the cause of political anarchy. 2. One who seeks to cause anarchy in the environment around him in pursuit of a political goal. Or perhaps an artistic goal. Or maybe just for the love of anarchy itself.

blesh: Sounds like something you'd do to tough stains, but actually is a word embraced by Bluemanologists, a combination of "blend" and "mesh." It describes the process of shedding one's ego in order to enter into a collective state of ecstasy or bliss. Leading Bluemanologists speculate that Blue Men experience this state up to a thousand times more daily than the human population.

Buster Keaton: A deadpan comic from the golden age of film comedy, notable for his deadpan humor. Bluemanologists are split as to whether the Blue Men influenced Keaton, or whether the similarity between Keaton and the Blue Men is a coincidence, sort of parallel evolution.

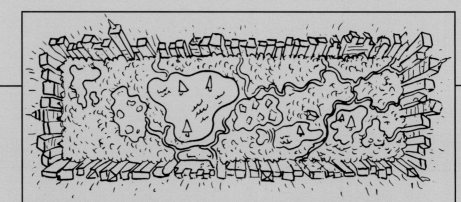

Central Park: That big park in the center of Manhattan.

colloid: A solution in which tiny particles of one substance are suspended inside another substance. Two different substances, coexisting, meshing without completely losing their individuality, proof that sometimes one plus one can equal three. Jell-O, for instance, is a liquid suspended in a solid, and also a third thing, a colloid. Three in one. When you talk about colloids they seem really pretentious, but in person they are a lot of fun.

deconstructionism: An ultra complex twentieth-century school of philosophy. It's related to structuralism and post-structuralizzz.

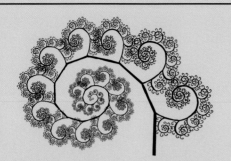

fractals: A mathematically generated image that graphically portrays how systems both degenerate and self-organize via self similarity, and that will wig you the eff out if you look at it too long.

Funeral for the Eighties: A ritualistic happening in New York in 1991, one of the first documented sightings of the Blue Men.

Funnelator: A device used in some Blue Man rituals. A giant slingshot used by the Blue Men to take aim at Jasper Johns's seminal masterpiece *Semiotics,* which, to be fair, looks a lot like a target.

hippie: A young, wide-eyed member of the counterculture from the mid-1960s onward. In the 1960s, hippie "likes" included psychedelics, communes, and free love. "Dislikes" included deodorant. Hippies were popular comic relief characters in movies of the sixties and seventies. They continue to haunt college dormitories everywhere.

Jell-O: An American dessert innovation, a mass-produced and mass-marketed version of the traditional English jelly or gelatin. Notable for its colorful translucence, reminiscent of a stained-glass window, and its wiggly jiggly wobbly squirmy squooshiness.

Kodo drummers: A professional troupe of taiko drummers from Japan, who have collaborated with Blue Man Group on joint rituals. A Kodo drummer's job is to hit an enormous drum really hard while looking like a total badass.

Kurt Loder: Former anchor of *MTV News.* He broke the story of a lifetime when he was the first in the mainstream media to "discover" the Blue Men.

life force: 1. A term used by Yves Klein in his *Anthropometry* series of paintings. 2. A term that tries really hard to get at the sense of the energy that flows through all of us; what is called qi by the Chinese, prana to Hindu practitioners, mana in Hawaiian culture, and the Force at Comic-Con. Some believe that the entire Blue Man ritual is an effort to summon up and harness life force.

Loki: Trickster god of Norse mythology, a shape-shifter. Like the Blue Men in that he is an unpredictable and slightly dangerous figure. Unlike the Blue Men in that he gave birth to the eight-legged horse Sleipnir.

Marx Brothers: A famous three-man comedy team active during the first half of the twentieth century, notable for wordplay and surrealist humor that seamlessly shifted between the prosaic and the sublime. Many suspect that silent partner, Harpo, was influenced by the Blue Men.

Moby: Well-known American musician, DJ, and photographer. Although he refuses to confirm or deny this, he is considered by many to be one of the nation's foremost "Blue Man Insiders," or emulators of the Blue Men. He founded the Area2 concert, which featured Blue Man Group.

Monty Python: A British comedy troupe active from the late sixties onward, characterized by absurdist and surreal humor, exuberant satire, and all-out silliness.

MTV: Music Television, an early cable television channel dedicated to music videos created exclusively to accompany a new song.

post-modern architecture: A school of architecture that defined much of the second half of the twentieth century. Post-modern buildings drew from previous schools of architecture to convey two messages at once. Sort of like "business casual," or "responsible but still likes to party."

open systems: 1. In systems theory, any system in which energy (or information or material) can enter from and exit to the outside. The term may apply equally to natural systems (such as ecosystems and organisms) as social systems (such as cities, or worldwide capitalist markets) or to information systems. 2. One of the many subjects we'd love to discuss with the Blue Men, if they could talk.

PVC: An instrument constructed from PVC piping and played by banging pipe openings. The love child of a pipe organ and the whack-a-mole game.

ritualistic happenings: In the early nineties, Blue Men were first spotted participating in events throughout New York City that are now referred to as "ritualistic happenings." Were the Blue Men attracted to happenings orchestrated by others? Or were they themselves instigating these events, preparing to build their greater ritual, which would someday reach the world? The questions remain unanswered.

Rambo: A troubled Vietnam vet eager to abandon the violence of war who is pushed into fighting again to protect himself and various innocents. The character, featured in numerous hugely popular Hollywood movies, turned his military training skills against the military.

Rambo-ism: A phenomenon in which an entire nation behaves like a high school bully, resorting to physical violence as a means to resolve complex issues.

shaman: A spiritual amphibian who can cross the boundaries between the physical and spirit world. Shamans may deliver messages to mere mortals, effect cures, or perform magical feats such as getting a skeptical crowd to shake their badonks.

rugged individualism: The idea that every person should be able to stand on their own, each man an island in a sea of . . . very densely packed islands.

three-as-one: 1. A mantra used by individuals, commonly referred to as Blue Man Insiders, who seek to follow the example of the Blue Men. 2. May also describe Aim® toothpaste, the Three Musketeers, or three children seated on each other's shoulders, dressed in a trench coat, impersonating a very tall man.

tribal: Of, or pertaining to, a tribe. A word sometimes used by Bluemanologists to describe Blue Man percussion and/or ritual aesthetic considered to be primal, evoking an ancient shared humanity that predates civilization. There are others who find this use of the word "tribal" problematic, evoking as it does the harmful old trope of the noble savage and a host of other colonialist ideas.

Vortex Machine: An artificial vortex (water spout) discovered in the antechamber to Blue Man Group's rituals. Emblematic of Blue Man Group's singular taste in interior decoration.

trickster: A comic archetype found in cultures around the world: the spirit of subversion, of anarchism, and of merry disrule. Like the shaman, the trickster is often considered an intermediary between humans and gods.

yuppie: A young urban professional, from the 1980s onward. In the 1980s, yuppie "likes" included sushi, expensive button-up shirts, and neon sculptures. "Dislikes" included living in one's hometown. Yuppies were popular villains in 1980s movies.

WHAT THE VORTEX MACHINES ARE TELLING US

BY CHRIS WINK

WE FIRST DECIDED TO BUILD the Vortex Machines because the image of a swirling funnel inside a Plexiglas cylinder resonated for us both viscerally and metaphorically. Viscerally, the vortex lent itself to the ritualistic primal yet industrial aesthetic we were aiming for. Metaphorically, we felt the vortex could represent the life force.

We had this idea after reading books on chaos theory. One of these books referred to whirlpools as simple open systems and humans as very complex ones. The author explained that, like all open systems, humans and whirlpool funnels can survive only as long as a constant stream of matter or energy flows through them. In the case of a whirlpool it's simple, water flows in and water flows out. Humans are a little more complicated but it's the same principle.

*"The open system known as a human being is always taking in energy and matter from the outside: food, light, oxygen, information; and it is always sending matter and energy back into the environment, in the form of carbon dioxide, waste, heat, art and other excretions."**

Art and other excretions. Now there's a good catchphrase. Anyway, from a chaos theory point of view, humans are really just slightly more complex, art-excreting whirlpools; and open systems "represent the conceptual link between nonlife and life."

After we built the Vortex Machines we found additional resonance. The millions of water molecules forming into a single funnel was consistent with our concept of "bleshing" (hybrid of "blend" and "mesh"), the merging of disparate elements into a collaborative whole. This is why we put them at the beginning of the show. When the Vortex Machines go on they serve as an emblem for what the Blue Men try to accomplish throughout the course of the evening; a three-as-one connection with each other, a six-as-one merging between Blue Men and band, and ultimately, a five-hundred-as-one "blesh" with the audience.

The swirling funnels represent a sort of poetic confluence; a tribe dancing around a fire, several minds working together to form a unique idea, an audience connected by paper. The funnel is a shift to a higher level of integration, the gestalt phenomenon.

The Vortex Machine also seems to work as a metaphor for the relationship between show and crew: a mesmerizing swirl of events onstage, driven by a hidden system below.

Recently, while rereading one of the old chaos theory books, I found a passage that had me focus for the first time on the moments between the time when the motor is turned on and when the funnel appears. It reminded me of something that we observed after Phil had just built several new Vortex Machines for a TV appearance: we noticed that freestanding Vortex Machines would come close to falling over right before the funnel formed.

The passage in the chaos book described the work of physicist, Ilya Prigogine, who won the Nobel Prize for his theories about special kinds of open systems called "dissipative structures." The author explained that one of the most interesting features of a dissipative structure is how it responds to sudden increases or decreases in the energy or matter flowing through it:

"Up to a certain point, the structure can absorb these fluctuations, dissipate the entropy, and still maintain its internal organization. For example, the human body can absorb a certain amount of electrical current with no real damage; it can cope with the loss of a limb or two; it can withstand a certain amount of impact or vibration without serious damage; it can suffer certain damages and still heal itself through its self-organizing capacity. A society is able to absorb the disruptions and instability caused by a minor war; it can suffer a moderate famine or drought and still 'heal' itself. Such fluctuations in a dissipative structure can, within limits, be absorbed.

At a certain point, though, the fluctuation begins to grow too great to be absorbed and healed, and the structure becomes more and more unstable. As the fluctuations increase, the structure reaches a critical point. It is highly unstable, like a complex machine that is on the verge or flying apart, maintaining its structure by the barest of margins. Perturbed by fluctuations, the elements of the system have increased interactions as they are brought into contact with other elements of the system in new ways. This razor's edge is the point where the system has the potential to move in an almost infinite variety of unpredictable directions, like an unstable society on the verge of revolution or a human at the crisis point of a severe disease. Like Saul of Taurus on the road to Damascus.

At this point even a small fluctuation can be sufficient to push the elements of the system beyond the point where they can heal themselves. Then suddenly the entire system seems to shudder and fall apart. In some cases the system may be destroyed. But if the system survives, it survives by emerging from this point of collapse (what Prigogine calls 'the bifurcation point') in a new pattern. The elements of the system, having increased their interactions with each other and been brought into contact with each other in novel ways, reorganize in a different form, create a new organization. This recombination of the elements of the system is essentially nonlinear, and the new level or organization is able to dissipate the entropy to the environment and maintain its new higher level of internal organization.

The nation that has undergone a revolution, with different levels of the society having been brought into contact with one another in new ways, creates a new government that is somehow able to absorb and dissipate the energy that had created the revolution in the earlier order of society. The human body creates new antibodies that are able to overcome a disease . . . Out of chaos emerges a transformed system; the dissipative structure has, in Prigogine's words, 'escaped into a higher order.' This higher order, once established, is stable, and resistant to further structural change or fluctuation."*

This is almost an exact description of the moments between when the Vortex Machine is turned on and when the funnel is formed. Here's my best attempt of describing what happens:

A sudden influx of energy is applied to the system by way of the propeller. The water absorbs this shock, but as the propeller spins on, the structure as a whole begins to feel its effects. The machine starts to shudder and shift in fits and starts while the water gurgles and hiccups. The motor strains, the water seems to resist, the structure starts to wobble. In this brief moment the whole machine is the image of instability, perturbation, and chaos. The wobbling turns into rocking, the hiccups into coughs. It clearly reaches a moment on the razor's edge where it is in danger of literally falling over (when not anchored to the stage). In this moment, it is completely unpredictable—fighting with itself, trying to find a way of dealing with this steady influx of energy that won't go away. It is nearing its bifurcation point. Then, out of nowhere, SWOOSH!, the funnel explodes into existence. Instantly the machine stops its wobbling—in fact, like a gyroscope, it is even more stable than before. The whalelike hum of a happy motor fills the room as the funnel spout executes its steady transcendent dance. The system, once on the verge of collapse, is now able to handle the new, higher level of energy flow.

Out of chaos has emerged a transformed system—the column of water has, in Prigogine's words, "escaped into a higher order."

Armed with Prigogine's model, we see that the vortex is much more than a metaphor. It is a tale of mythic proportions—a story that tells us that the process of transformation to a higher order is not without risk—that the same energy flow that can bring about an elegant, transcendent funnel can also lead to a wipeout if not properly channeled. It illustrates that the process itself is nonlinear and what scientists call "salutary," that is, "characterized by sudden leaps and discontinuities rather than gradual incremental progressions." It tells us, as Prigogine points out, that "periods of instability, perturbation, upheaval, and chaos are not to be seen as absolute evils, but instead as phases through which every structure must pass in order to evolve to higher levels of complexity."

As we move into the next phase of development at Blue Man we would do well to remember the vortex. Our goal right now is to create a new level of systemic integration and more unity of vision and purpose throughout the company. As a community, we are trying to find the funnel.

The vortex tells us that anything short of powerful, sustained, focused energy will be futile. Imagine how ineffective and intermittent, varying speed or weak motor would be in coaxing a funnel into existence.

But the vortex also tells us something that is somewhat counterintuitive: we will never get there if we pull back when things get a little off balance. Imagine turning the vortex off after only a few seconds because it started to look unstable. The paradox is this: Unless we are willing to push through the harrowing bifurcation point we will never reach a higher level of stability.

And because this process is not incremental it will not always be clear if our efforts are moving us closer.

If we ever get confused about how it works we should return to what we know—to what we do every night: turn the motor on full and leave it on, turn up the volume and hold on tight—

THE FUNNEL WILL SHOW UP.

*All quotes from *Mega Brain: Evolution Against Entropy*, by Michael Hutchinson, Ballantine Books, 1986

THE ORIGINS OF THE BLUE MAN INSIDERS MOVEMENT CAN BE TRACED DIRECTLY BACK TO THREE FRIENDS—

Some researchers claim the trio have established a creative collective dedicated to the continued exploration of the Blue Man character, including the practical application of their interpretations and findings.

Evidence proving the existence of this creative collective is under review.

However, it is commonly accepted that the trio have garnered the most extensive experience and expertise in the field of Blue Man studies.

PHIL STANTON

CHRIS WINK

AND

MATT GOLDMAN

THANK YOU

THERE IS NO BLUE MAN WITHOUT THE GROUP.

This book came together thanks to the contributions of many, including the creative teams and administrative staff who support every Blue Man Group project, the dedicated teams of people who create the Blue Man happenings around the world every night, and the legions of fans who attend them.

WE APPRECIATE YOU AND WE THANK YOU.

Special thanks to our co-founders **CHRIS WINK, PHIL STANTON, & MATT GOLDMAN** for "finding" the Blue Men.

Our utmost thanks and appreciation to all those new to the Blue Man World who contributed in so many ways: endlessly patient and wise editor **BECKY KOH**; design advisor and book doula **PETE FRIEDRICH**; our design sorcerers **BONNIE SIEGLER, ANDREW JAMES CAPELLI,** and **KRISTEN REN**; our fantastic agent **JIM LEVINE** and the entire team at **LEVINE, GREENBERG AND ROSTAN**.

To all the artists and photographers whose commissioned work adds beauty and depth to our book— (SEE FULL LIST ON PHOTO CREDITS PAGE).

To all the company members past and present who opened their archives and shared their personal photography with us: **ADAM ZUICK, ALEXANDER BRUEHL, AMANDA CLAYTON, ANDREW PLUMMER, ANITA SHAH, ANNIE LOWRIE, ANTHONY SCHUTZ, BILL SWARTZ, BONNIE SNOWDEN, BRIAN TAVENER, CATHERINE CALLAHAN, CARYL GLAAB, CHARLES GARLAND, CHRIS NAKA, CORKY GAINSFORD, DAN COOPER, DAN GREEN, DAN MATAS, DAVE STEELE, DESTINY PAQUETTE, ED GREGORY, ENDERLEE PARIS, GARETH DAVID HINSLEY, GEOFF GERSH, JAMIA GAFFNEY, JEFF TORTORA, JEFFREY BROWN, JOJO DRAVEN, JONATHAN MARTIN, JOY CLELAND, JULIA TORRES, JULIE DAUBER, LAURA CAMIEN, LISE RASMUSSEN, MARK FRANKEL, MARCUS ROSS, MEAGAN BECKER, MIKE SAVAGE, NANCY FELDMAN, NAYON KIM, PETE SIMPSON, RANDY WOOTEN, ROBERT SIMRING, ROSIE GOLDMAN, SARAH GARRETT, SCOTT DAHL, SCOTT FINLAYSON, SCOTT SPEISER, SHAWN GRESSER, STEPHANIE SPANGLER, TAMMY UNGLESBEE, TODD WAETZIG, TOM GALASSI, VINCE VERDERAME, WADE ELKINS**

And so many more whose support and contributions throughout the process made this book possible: **DOUG BALDINGER, STEVE BALLSTADT, JOHN BARFIELD, ZEA BARKER, KERRY CONCANNON, DEVIN CONWAY, MOHAMED DAWANI, WES DAY, CAMILLE DEPASCALE, KIRVIN DOAK COMMUNICATIONS, CHRIS DYAS, LLOYD EDELMAN, SHEA ELMORE, BEN FLINT, CARYL GLAAB, ALLIE GRANT, MARY GRISOLANO, CATHLEEN HENKER, JOAN HILTY, MADELINE HOLMES, PETER HOLMES, ALEX HORWITZ, BRUCE HUANG, HAILEY JESTER, COURTNEY KING, JAQUELINE KOLEK, ALAN LEVEY, TERRI MARUCA, CHASE MAYO, CHANDRA MCCLELLAND, BENTLEY MEEKER, ANNALISA MICKELSON, MARCUS MILLER, DESTINY PAQUETTE, GINA PAYTON, BABITA PERSAUD, RICH PHILLIS, KORI PRIOR, JEN QUINONEZ, CAREY RANDALL, STACY RAVE, JOHN ROGERS, MIKE SAVAGE, ANDREW SCHNEIDER, BRAD SEIDEL, RACHEL SIEGEL, STEPHANIE SPANGLER, FOPPE TALMAN, KARA THORNTON, JOE TROPIA, MICHELLE TROTMAN, LEAH TUCKER, JEFF TURLIK**

EXTRA SPECIAL THANKS

To the Blue Man 'Insiders' whose intimate knowledge of the Blue Man character and the soulful way that they conjure him forward continues to entertain and inspire us all:

SHANECA ADAMS KALEN ALLMANDINGER SHANE ANDRIES GREG BALLA MATTHEW BANKS GIDEON BANNER CHAD BANTNER MARTIN BERMOSER AURELIAN BERNARD SCOTT BISHOP LYLE BLAKER PATRICK BRANSTETTER CHRIS BOWEN DAVID BRAY MIKE BROWN CHRIS BROWN JEFFREY BROWN ZACK BUELL ANDREW BURLINSON ANDREW CALVERT MICHAEL CATES ERIC CHERNEY EKE CHUKWU JONATHAN "MERIDIAN" CLAPHAM RICHARD CRAVENS DAN COOPER MICHAEL DAHLEN BRENDAN DALTON WES DAY ERIC DELIMA RUBB KARL DOBBY JEFFREY DOORNBOS ISAAC EDDY ERAY EGILMEZ WADE ELKINS JOSH ELROD ADAM ERDOSSY DUSTIN FONTAINE BEN FORSTER MARK FRANKEL DAVID GADDIS TOM GALASSI ISAAC GARDNER ERIC GEBOW YANN GEOFFROY RYAN GERARD JASON GILBERT JEREMY GILL BRETT GILLEN ZACH GLASS MATT GOLDMAN ETHAN GOLUB JOHN GRADY CALLUM GRANT ULI GREWE ADAM GRIFFIN BARNEY HAAS JAKE HART JOHN HARTZEL TIM HECK ARIEL HELLER NADIM HELOW GARETH DAVID HINSLEY COLIN HURD RANDALL JAYNES GENERAL JUDD SCOTT KINWORTHY NICHOLAS KITTLE DAN KOHLER CHRISTOPHER LAVENDER FRANK LICARI STEFAN LIDEN JASON LONG JIM LUDWIG MARTIN MARION JAMES MARLOWE KIRK MASSEY VINICIUS MASTEGUIM DAVID MCLAUGHLIN JASON MCLIN RONAN MCMAHON CHRIS MENDEZ ANDREW ELVIS MILLER DAVID MUELLER PETER MUSANTE PATRICK NEWTON FEMI OYEWOLE ANTHONY PARRULLI KUBA PIERZCHALSKI NICK PILARSKI RICK PLAUGHER FELIX POWROSLO THOM RACKETT DENNIS RADELAAR MICHAEL RAHHAL MATT RAMSEY RUSSELL RINKER MARC ROBERTS ALAIN ROCHEFORT TAHMUS ROUNDS NICK RUSH SEUMAS SARGENT DANIEL SCHROEDER BRIAN SCOTT BHURIN SEAD MATT SHALLENBERGER PETE SIMPSON BENEDICT SMITH CHRIS SMITH ALEX SOEHNLE BRYCE SOMERVILLE SCOTT SPEISER PHIL STANTON PIET STARRETT BRIAN TAVENER SHAWN STURNICK OLE SÜNDERMAN CASEY SWEENEY JONATHAN TAYLOR KRISTIAN THORSON LAURENS WALTER MARCUS WEISS STEVEN WENDT NATHAN WETHERINGTON STEVE WHITE RESTON WILLIAMS CHRIS WINK JORDAN WOODS-ROBINSON JOE WOOLMER ADAM ZUICK

BLUE MAN WORLD BOOK TEAM

EXECUTIVE PRODUCERS:
CHRIS WINK, PHIL STANTON, LES KELLEY,
PAM HARRIS

CREATIVE DIRECTOR AND HEAD WRITER:
LAURA CAMIEN

CREATIVE PRODUCER:
MEGAN KINGERY

ART DIRECTION AND DESIGN:
BONNIE SIEGLER, ANDREW JAMES CAPELLI,
EIGHT AND A HALF

EDITOR:
BECKY KOH, BLACK DOG & LEVENTHAL

PRINCIPLE DESIGN ADVISOR AND CURATOR:
PETE FRIEDRICH, PAGETURNER

ADDITIONAL DESIGN ADVISORS AND CURATORS:
CHRIS WINK, PHIL STANTON, BILL SWARTZ,
DAVID STEELE, CARYL GLAAB, MAX FREY,
JON KNIGHT, CHRIS NAKA

CONTRIBUTING WRITERS:
CHRIS WINK, PHIL STANTON, SARAH GANCHER,
MICHAEL QUINN, ARIELLE ECKSTUT AND DAVID HENRY
STERRY (THE BOOK DOCTORS), MICHAEL DAHLEN,
CHRISTOPHER BOWEN, BRIAN SCOTT, MEGAN KINGERY,
BILL SWARTZ, DAVID STEELE, MATT RAMSEY,
RANDALL JAYNES, TIM AUMILLER, BYRON ESTEP

LEGAL COUNSEL AND BUSINESS AFFAIRS:
LYDIA CHEUK

IMAGE CREDITS

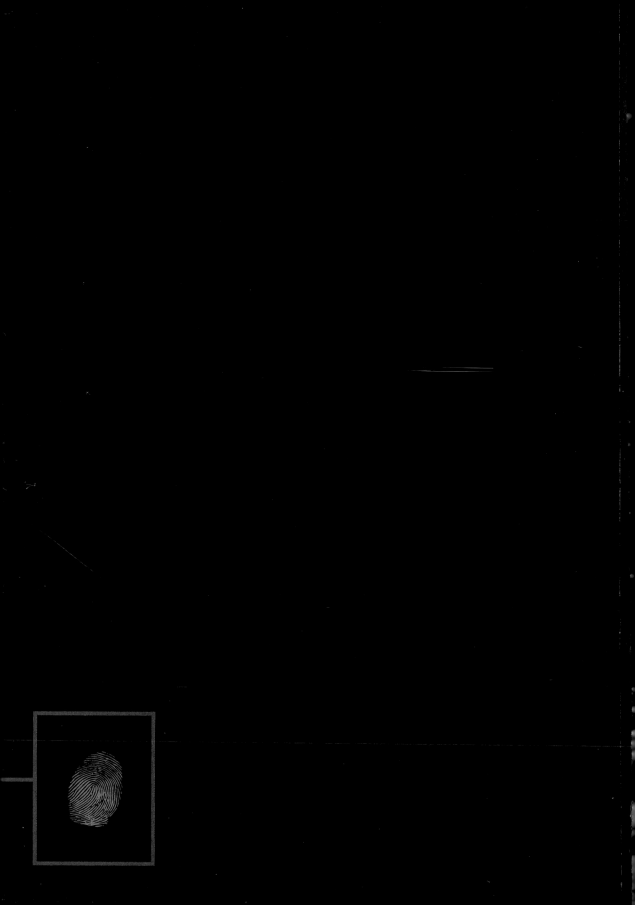